Scourge of Cords

Driving the moneychangers out of the temple!

Scourge of Cords

"And when He had made a scourge of small cords He
drove them all out of the temple . . . and
poured out the changer's money,
and overthrew the tables."

---John, chapter 2, verse 15

2009
Aquila Press, Inc.

Order this book online at www.trafford.com
or email orders@trafford.com

Most Trafford titles are also available at major online book retailers.

Request for permission should be addressed to Aquila Press.
1350 South 9th Street, Noblesville, Indiana 46060
This is first edition published by Trafford Publishing.
Co-published by Aquila Press Inc. and Trafford Publishing.

Note for Librarians: A cataloguing record for this book is available from Library
and Archives Canada at www.collectionscanada.ca/amicus/index-e.html

Printed in Victoria, BC, Canada.

ISBN: 978-1-4269-1788-2

*Our mission is to efficiently provide the world's finest, most comprehensive book publishing
service, enabling every author to experience success. To find out how to publish your
book, your way, and have it available worldwide, visit us online at www.trafford.com*

Trafford rev. 09/30/09

 www.trafford.com

North America & international
toll-free: 1 888 232 4444 (USA & Canada)
phone: 250 383 6864 ♦ fax: 812 355 4082

Contents

Introduction – 9

~1~ The Enigma of "money" – 18

~2~ An Elementary view of "money" – 21

~3~ Debt-merchants and their bags of gold -- 26

~4~ The Final Stroke – 34

~5~ Genesis of private banking – 38

~6~ Money based on debt – 41

~7~ Founding Fathers – 44

~8~ Lincoln's "greenbacks" – 47

~9~ Usurers move with a vengeance – 51

~10~ "On a cross of gold" – 55

~11~ The "Fed" – 60

~12~ Father of the "Lone Eagle" – 68

~13~Corporate influence – 73

~14~ Bankers testify under oath – 77

15~ "Primer on Money" – 81

~16~ Boom and Bust – 96

~17~ Debt and Vampiristic interest – 101

~18~ 9-inch ball of gold -- 109

~19~ Sage of Menlo Park – 113

~20~The human tragedy – 120

~21~"Wealth, Virtual Wealth and Debt" – 127

~22~ World Connections – 134

~23~ Summary -- 143

~24~ "Greatest crime in history!" – 151

~25~H.R. 17140 -- 160

~26~Enlightenment – 168

~27~Private banking control of the
Nation's money and credit -- 173

~28~Pattern for Political Slavery – 176

~29~Taming of Science and Technology -- 184

~30~Proposals—189

~31~A sense of direction-- 193

~32~ This land is our land – 198

~33~Retrieving the people's wealth -- 201

~34~Cornerstones of the Commonwealth ~ 204

~35~Equal human rights – 208

~36~Functioning of the Commonwealth – 212

~37~Determing Individual Worth – 218

~38~Two other important agencies – 221

~39~End of private banking – 224

40~Department of Housing – 231

~41~Peace with economic justice – 236

~42~ Collaborating with tyrants -- 240

~43~ World War II – 248

~44~ Continuous Wars – 258

~45~ Project for a new American Century—261

~46~ Power and Morality – 266

~47~ Action – 270

~48~ Inauguration of a National Cooperative
Commonwealth – 275

Bibliography – 279

Index – 283-291

Money is the creature of law, and the creation of the original issue of money should be maintained as an exclusive monopoly of the Nation's Government. . . The privilege of creating and issuing money is not only the supreme prerogative of the Government; it is the Government's greatest opportunity.

----- Abraham Lincoln

Introduction

I was born to Scandinavian parents in northern Minnesota on August 1, 1916. When I was four years old, my father died from incurable tuberculosis, leaving my mother in her late twenties with a brood of five little ones to be fed and clothed, and each Saturday night to be lined up for their weekly bath. In later years, we enjoyed the exclusive status of being members of the "tin-tub club." Along with candles and kerosene lamps, they were the state of the art in achieving both cleanliness and insight.

By the time I graduated from high school in 1934, I had become aware of the interests and political astuteness of my father. To this day I am appreciative of the fact that I had been born into the right family at the right time. Looking over my father's library, I became aware of his being a follower of Eugene V. Debs, national labor organizer, political activist and one who gained notorious recognition when he campaigned as the Socialist presidential candidate from a prison cell.

In addition my father took great pride in being an admirer and supporter of Minnesota's Congressman, Charles A. Lindbergh Sr., who was the father of the "Lone Eagle" who achieved world renown for the first solo flight across the Atlantic.

Realizing my father's strong belief in Lindbergh's stand in Congress, especially his heroic and courageous fight against the enactment of the Federal Reserve Act, I was eager to read some of his books. I soon was reading his book **Banking and Currency and the Money Trust,** his book **My Country at War** and his campaign material when he ran for governor.

Despite the fact that I was still in my teens, it seemed providential that I was holding material in my hands that resonated so strongly in my thinking. Perhaps the fact that "money," the lack of it, was a real family problem, along with my acute awareness that millions were suffering the worst economic depression that the nation had ever endured, made my interest in banking and economics so compelling and relevant.

By the time I was seventeen, I had read not only Congressman Lindbergh's books but had become acquainted with his battle on the floor of Congress opposing the setting up of a Central Bank in this nation patterned after the banking systems in Europe.

At the time of my graduation from high school, the peak of the Great Depression had come upon the nation with one-third of the nation ill-fed, ill-housed and ill-clothed. I was one of the twenty million able-bodied men who were futilely seeking employment. While I did have scholarships to several colleges, I forewent them in order to assist my widowed mother in providing for the basic needs of the family.

Many questions arose in my inquiring mind. The primary one, as it is today, questioned what were the barriers preventing the nation from unleashing its full work capability to solve all its major problems, particularly poverty? How could you have such dire human needs, children crying for food, and at the same time have the capability to meet those needs?

Other puzzling questions came to mind, which perplexed and haunted me. Why were the farmers being forced off their farms by foreclosures when they worked so hard from morning to night in the planting and harvesting of their crops? Hadn't they fulfilled their job of providing the nation with an abundance of food and fiber?

What sense did it make for the government to contend that the nation suffered from overproduction when at the same time tens of millions were going to bed hungry and tens of millions were ill clothed and ill-housed?

And then the insanity of the government's answer! A program was initiated to slaughter one-third of all pigs, and plow under every third row of corn and cotton. The government's agricultural programs were nonsensical and criminal in terms of sheer destruction.

The approach to the unemployed was just as illogical. Instead of giving gainful work to the millions without jobs to build decent homes for the one-third of the population who were ill-housed, and provide work to replace or repair the nation's infrastructure, a whole series of relief programs were initiated that were demeaning and largely a waste of constructive effort.

Something was drastically wrong with the whole private capitalist economic system. There was work that needed to be done. There were able-bodied men and willing hands to do all necessary tasks. All the ingredients, natural resources, workers, machinery and technical know-how were present to meet all the requirements of the people. Something was preventing their combining to meet abundantly the needs of the society.

The nation faced an enigma!

It was here that the thinking of Congressman Lindbergh rang such a resounding bell. It was his analysis of private banking and his focusing on concentrated corporate "money trusts" that gave me real insight to the dilemma that beset the nation. I came to understand the unconstitutional status of private banking and the strangling effect it had on the economy.

Basic questions came to mind. What was this incredible power that was lodged in the hands of private financial institutions? How did the Federal Reserve System function in making interest-bearing loans and subsequently wresting the farms and homes from their owners when they couldn't repay the loans through no fault of their own?

Why should private institutions be given life-and-death despotic control over the economic lives of the people? And over the people's government!

Congressman Lindbergh had provided answers to the whole enigma of private banking. They instilled in me a lifetime of challenging the abusive role it played in the lives of the people. I came to understand the unconstitutionality of the Federal Reserve Act and over the years I witnessed a constant struggle for economic security against a persistent onslaught of mushrooming indebtedness, both public and private.

Incredible, as it may seem, today we face the same serious problems of millions in poverty, millions without work, millions mentally breaking under the pressures of an aberrated society. However, the situation is much graver. Increasingly, through "globalization" and unchecked mergers multi-nationals have despotically taken over the work capability of the nation, to the detriment of the people both nationally and internationally

Ominously, and recklessly, the United States has gravitated to the role that it is destined to be dominant over the whole world. Slowly, and methodically, this imperialistic role emerged openly and took blatant shape under the Administration of George W. Bush. As the mightiest military nation in the world "we" have assumed the right, irrespective of international law and obligations under the United Nations Charter, to seek "regime change" whenever we find the rulers of others nations not to our liking.

A "unilateral preemptive-strike doctrine" has been adopted that bodes most serious consequence into the future when other nations feel an equal right to adopt a similar doctrine. Currently, it has landed us in the quagmire of Iraq with American service men and women dying every day with no solution in the offing.

Grasping the wrongs of private banking was only half the picture that my mind grappled with during those formative years during the early 1930s. Another penetrating insight was to come to my attention. It strangely came to me by a friend of the family who brought a copy of a magazine that carried a most intriguing advertisement that caught my attention.

It suggested that one send for a copy of **No More Hunger** and learn how the nation could be set aright by incorporating the entire economy into what was called a "Christian Commonwealth." Not only would an equitable, participatory society emerge but within the economic framework the whole problem of interest-bearing indebtedness would be solved.

William Dudley Pelley, nationally known writer of fiction stories and novels, and a scenario writer in Hollywood where two of his novels were made into movies, was the author of **No More Hunger.** He was also the founder of a philosophical movement called "Liberation Soulcraft," and was the author of over 20 books on metaphysical subjects.

During the 1930s he was the stormy petrel that challenged the wrongs in our society. He became a friend of Congressman Louis T. McFadden, Chairman of the *House Committee on Banking and Currency*, and cooperated with him in exposing the wrongs of the Federal Reserve System.

I would be remiss if I didn't note the controversial sequence of his life in which he was charged and convicted of "sedition" and spent seven and a half years of a 15-year sentence in prison. This aspect of Mr. Pelley's life as the nation's outstanding political prisoner of the Twentieth Century will be referred to when we deal with the deceit and political, maneuvering that embroiled us in WWII.

Suffice here to state that Mr. Pelley seriously opposed our entry into WWII. He contended that by letting Germany and the Soviet Union destroy themselves the United States would be in a strong role of leadership in negotiating differences between nations. His legal difficulties were immense and costly.

More costly was, of course, the loss of **fifty three million** lives in a war that could have been prevented!

The main "evidence" used against Mr. Pelley was his expose of Sovietism and his opposition to the formal recognition of the Soviet Union under Joseph Stalin. All his projected warnings, after we became allied with the Soviet Union, were used against him on the twisted conclusion that they tended to cause "disloyalty in our **combined** leadership."

During his incarceration he was also included, along with some thirty other defendants, in the so-called "Mass Sedition Trial" in the nation's capitol. Despite the Constitutional prohibition of "double jeopardy" the same evidence was used against him the second time. In 1946 Chief Justice Bolitha Laws of the Federal Court in Washington, DC, threw the whole case out citing that it would be a "travesty on justice" to permit the case to continue.

Up until 1965, when Mr. Pelley passed on, no court would rejudicate the original conviction in Indianapolis giving legal consideration to the Supreme Court decisions which prompted the dismissal of the Mass Sedition Case.

There is solid reasoning to believe that the real "crime" that Mr. Pelley committed was to advance the proposals of his book **No More Hunger,** which would eradicate the usurped power of the Federal Reserve System.

It was my good fortune to marry Mr. Pelley's daughter, Adelaide, and in the 1940s we worked together seeking her father's release from durance vile. The experience in the nation's capitol was immeasurable in learning the ropes and machinations of the nation's political processes.

In 1961, Adelaide, my brother and I incorporated Aquila Press, Inc. to document the corporate takeover, both financial and non-financial, of the nation's work capability. At the same time we promoted the idea of a **National Cooperative Commonwealth.**

We changed the name "Christian Commonwealth" to a "National Cooperative Commonwealth" as we felt that the Idea was one that should appeal and be adopted by every segment of the society irrespective of religious affiliation. The copyright to **No More Hunger** was turned over to us and we had the blessing of Mr. Pelley to make that change.

We published a monthly magazine, *The Eagles Eye,* during the 1960s in which both our documentation of corporate, monopolistic take-over, and an assertive promotion of the "Commonwealth Idea" made up its pages. Out of our exhaustive research, I wrote my first book **Challenge to Crisis** published in 1969.

In 1995, I wrote **There is A Way!** to focus on how all the proposals of the Commonwealth could legally be brought about within the framework of the Constitution.

In 2003, I wrote **A Blueprint for Survival** against the background of "downsizing," with the loss of millions of jobs, increased violence in our own nation, the mounting hatred for our nation throughout the world and the imperialistic doctrine of "unilateral pre-emptive strike".

While I had noted the iniquities of the Federal Reserve System in all three books, I felt that I should devote a book that mainly focused on private banking and its devastating role in our society.

Initially the documented treatment of the Federal Reserve System might appear harsh to some readers. However, I know that when the reader grasps the pervasive economic suffering it has caused since it became the law of the land, my indictment will seem too mild.

In writing my other books I have underscored that I am not indicting the workers in the banking system. My concern is to indict the **system itself** as flawed and ruinous to the nation's well being.

The same perspective must be entertained relative to every occupation and role in our capitalist society. We are all victims, irrespective of being a CEO or one on welfare. Hopefully, we can all rally around national change that will make the entire society secure, equitable and abundantly prosperous.

Many years have passed since I first got interested in private banking and the abusive functioning of the Federal Reserve System. Its genesis started with Congressman Lindbergh's books that occupied so prominent a position in my father's library.

Melford Pearson

February 4, 2009

1

The enigma of "money"

SEVERAL economists were pondering the economic problems besetting the nation. Why were there tens of millions of people enduring poverty when store shelves were overflowing with an abundance of food and 40% of all farm products were exported? What justification could be given for twelve million children going to bed each night suffering the pangs of hunger?

Why was there an inability to build the necessary low-income houses, update medical institutions and repair unsafe schools? Why could not the nation replace its whole infrastructure that was in such critical need of attention?

And, why did the government and the people become increasingly burdened by trillions of dollars in indebtedness, a constant flow of business and farm foreclosures, when progressively they developed greater and greater means to produce all goods and services?

There seemed an endless list of questions to be answered in order to achieve economic stability, erase needless suffering and create a just and non-violent society. . . .

As the economists pondered without answers to the nation's dilemma, they suddenly became aware of the presence of a stranger who seemed to have overheard the discussion of the quandary. Without the stranger introducing himself, it was obvious that his demeanor and speech were not that of this planet. He was gentle in his inquiry:

"Is your inability to produce all your needs a lack of natural resources?"

"No, we have an abundance of resources. God has blessed us with a surfeit of soil, minerals, forests, water and air for our use."

"How about workers?"

"Workers? No lack. Beside those working, we have a pool of workers, skilled and unskilled, who are idle and without employment."

"How about machines?"

In responding to this question, the economists were slightly hesitant because they knew that their answer would seem incredible in light of the staggering evolution of machines in production, services and communication, when at the same time the nation had so many unmet human needs. However, the question was one that must be answered.

"We have great pride in our history's accomplishments in the evolutionary development of machines, technology and ever advancing scientific knowledge. From the simple use of hand tools and a strong back, we have witnessed major strides in the application of power to machines, the adoption of the assembly line, the introduction of automation, cybernation and finally computerization. Our capability to do work has been multiplied a thousand-fold."

The stranger was somewhat taken aback by the impact of this reply and the potential of machines to do work. He posed his final question with a slight note of bewilderment.

"If you have a plentitude of natural resources, and you have an oversupply of workers, skilled and unskilled, and you have a mechanical-technological capability that can bring into being an over-abundance of both goods and services, is there some other tangible ingredient that is missing?"

Somewhat sheepishly, the economists were forced to reply, "No, there is no other tangible ingredient that is missing."

"Then, pray, what is missing?" the stranger pointedly asked.

The answer to this final question came without hesitation. "We do not have the necessary "money."

The stranger was moved to recap the whole picture. "If I understand you gentlemen correctly, you have all the basic ingredients necessary to do all the things you need to do to make your nation healthy and enjoyable, but your only lack is an intangible thing called "money" that contributes nothing to the actual goods and services you want to provide for the people. Is that your problem?"

No matter how the economists tried, they were unable to explain how the nation had become subservient to a thing called "money" and why they paid tribute to non-producers who issued and controlled it. . . .

As the stranger departed, he turned and gave a final glance at the puzzled economists, and as he disappeared in the distance, he was seen to shake his head in utter disbelief. . . .

2

An Elementary view of "money"

THIS SMALL BOOK will try and unmask the mystery of money and private banking. Hopefully, it will answer the questions that the economists pondered. And, some day, by chance, it might fall into the hands of the visiting stranger that he might know there were those who did understand the strangling role of the nation's debt-merchants.

When we come to consider private banking institutions and their issuance of the nation's money supply and credit, we deal with operations largely hidden and enshrouded in mystery. It is a function least understood by the American people, and yet it is a function that impinges more seriously on everyone's life than any other economic force in our society.

How strange that the average person evinces so little interest in **what** is money, **how** it is created and **who** creates it. Despite such lack of inquiry, there is no item more desperately sought for each waking hour of the day. He or she will work until aching muscles prevent sleep, will work at two jobs, will embezzle or steal, will even kill under extreme pressure, and all the while show a complete disinterest as to **what** money is and **who** creates it. Why is there such indifference?

Foremost is the fact that it has been in the self-interest of those who profit most from the manipulation and control of the nation's money and credit to keep the people in ignorance. Another reason is that the people give thought, or are exposed, to the subject of "money" only in association with the intricate ramifications of banking, and its statistics, and they are quickly bored and confused by the labyrinth of detail expressed in banking jargon.

A third reason is perhaps the strongest influence in causing disinterest and timidity. Any person who is brash enough to question the honesty and workability of our monetary system is immediately stigmatized as being an advocate of "funny money" or more seriously finds that he or she is no longer a welcome patron at the local banking institution.

In an economy whose supply of money and credit is wholly dependent on debt-money, the latter reprisal can be devastating to either businessperson or wage-earning citizen!

FIRST, let us deal with the question of what is money. While our presentation might seem unnecessarily elementary, it is only in considering the subject in a rudimentary approach that we can fully comprehend what its role **is** and what its role **should be.**

Walk up to the average person, either worker or consumer, and ask him or her to give you a definition of "money" and surprisingly, despite their dearth of understanding about the whole subject, will give a very accurate response. He or she will blurt out something to the effect, "All I know is that it will buy anything I want." Of course, there will be a few additional expressions relating to the difficulty of acquiring the elusive stuff.

Slightly modifying the foregoing response we come up with this definition: **Money is anything that people will accept in exchange for goods and services, in the belief that they may in turn exchange it, now**

or later, for other goods or services. In short, it is any "medium of exchange" that is acceptable to all people. Or another way of expressing it is to say that money in whatever acceptable form simply facilitates barter.

A farmer will exchange his bushels of wheat or truckload of cattle for a **check**, which he in turn can exchange for machinery. The professional person will likewise exchange services for a check or **currency,** that "green-stuff", which in turn can be exchanged for sporting equipment.

And the same holds true for the millions of workers who exchange their labor for wages, in either checks or currency, and in turn can exchange such "money" for groceries, down-payment on a new station wagon, diapers for the new baby, and for a thousand and one things having to do with maintaining a household and raising a family.

For all small purchases coin (pennies, nickels, dimes, quarters, half-dollars and dollars) is employed. If we add coins to currency and checks (including all forms of credit cards), we have covered for all practical purposes the basic forms of "money" that make up our nation's money supply.

We only have to add one qualification to money, that it is "legal tender" and will be accepted in payment of taxes, and for both public and private debts, and we have described money.

We have described money, but we have not explained it.

To DO SO, we must start with simple barter. This process not only existed during earliest recorded history but also to a large extent held true during the beginning of our own nation. For reasons that will become graphically clear to us later we will understand why the return to barter at the present time is so eagerly adopted in many communities of the nation. Barter is simply the exchange of both goods and services between individuals.

Beginning in the nation's earliest history, one person who had too much of one product would trade it to another person for a product, which that person in turn had to surfeit. Or the exchange was prompted only by the desire to possess what the other owned. All parties gained directly from such exchange and there was no loss of value except when shrewd traders were able to drive hard bargains.

Even as societies became more complex, and distance became a factor in the exchange of the growing number of products, an advanced form of barter still provided the method of exchange. People came to accept some product, because of its universal use, as a unit by which all other products and services could be valued and exchanged.

Thus, in our own colonial days a number of commodities were used as money. Tobacco was primarily used in the southern states while various products such as coon-skins, whisky, corn, rice and timber were used elsewhere.

Right here a most important observation must be made in understanding the whole question, or mystery, of money. When you have simple barter, either by direct exchange of products, or in terms of some universally usable product, there exists an exchange of intrinsic or earned values. No one loses. The coonskins, the tobacco, the timber, or any other product, represent wealth to be exchanged for other wealth.

It is when we consider "money" beyond simple barter that we commence to grapple with a medium of exchange that is not directly related to products and services. All kinds of problems and inequities arise to stymie economies and prevent the people from enjoying the fruits of their labor.

A nation's money supply is the bloodstream of the nation and everything that dilutes it, or contaminates it, or obstructs its natural flow, interferes with the economic well-being of a total citizenry. We need to unmask the mysteries and inherent flaws of private banking. More importantly, we need to understand the elements and dynamics of an honest and workable money system. .

~ 3 ~

Debt-merchants and their bags of gold

LET US CONJURE up an island community. On this island are 100 inhabitants who are engaged in various occupations producing all the goods and services needed by all the islanders. Not having heard of private bankers, and their deceptive persuasion that no economy can function without money based on some mystical metal or on interest-bearing indebtedness, they have merely chosen the one amongst them who is most adept at keeping records.

He is designated as the island's accountant-treasurer, but at the same time is considered as having the same status as any other worker performing a service.

At all times our island's "banker" keeps a record of the earned contributions of each person to the total goods and services which the full employment of the islanders make available for purchase. To each person, including himself, he issues "contribution-claims," carrying the official seal of the island's government. The total of the claims constitute the island's money supply.

Our first observation should be obvious. In the possession of the inhabitants is a total money supply, or purchasing power, that is not only directly related to the producing and consuming needs of the people, but is at the same time **equal** to the **total** goods and services that are purchasable.

The second observation is of equal significance. The claims came into existence as **work was done**. The islanders didn't first have to get their hands on some external source of "money" in order to perform work and advance their wellbeing. Claims came into existence automatically as human effort was expended.

The claims were simply unit-measurements of human effort and the total unit-claims were always equal to the goods and services that were produced. The island had a sound and adequate "money system." And the island community prospered in direct ratio to its productive capability.

Our hypothetical island has been kept purposely simple so as to accentuate the basic relationships of a community's money supply to its producing, rewarding and consuming needs.

How to democratically negotiate the relative worth of each citizen, thus determining the purchasing income of each, and also the price-cost of all goods and services, would serve no purpose at this point. It will be dealt with, along with public services, when we consider the major renovations within a national economic framework that must be embraced.

We deliberately conjured up our island community in order to portray a society in which all the "money" in circulation were **earned claims**. We wanted you to grasp that the origin and issue of money should be the absolute function of a sovereign people through their government, and that the compensation for a nation's banking service should be based solely on the expenses incurred as with any other public service.

Right here we want to interject the private banker into our island-community and see what happens when **unearned claims** are the source of the money supply.

Of course, we will have to assume that the islanders succumbed to the age-old deceit that it is not only unsound for a sovereign people to issue and control their own money supply but that the only sound money is one which is based on a mystic metal called "gold" and on private and public "interest-bearing indebtedness."

If the islanders had not been foggy of mind and mesmerized to believe that private bankers were peculiarly indispensable, they would have asked a most pertinent question: How come the bankers, who are not producers but only have their bags of gold which have no literal bearing on our island's needs or enjoyment, can create purchasing power to compete with our "contribution-claims" for which we have expended much effort?

Tragically, the question was not forthcoming for the bankers had addressed the islanders most deceptively and cunningly.

"You poor benighted islanders! You do not have an historically proven banking system. You have made a great mistake by providing for your own money supply. We bankers have a long history of tried and established practices. We are skilled in the use of the tools of our profession. And we possess the gold of the world, which is the only basis for sound money. How ridiculous of you to believe that you could issue money into circulation without either incurring a debt or without the charge of interest!

"Of course, you should concern yourselves with government and the making of laws (the islanders missed the obscured wink exchanged by the bankers) but all matters dealing with money must be independent of government and entrusted only to private bankers.

With your current unconventional banking practice you have become the victims of the advocates of "funny money" who have tampered with tradition and the "divine right" of usurers. In the past we have always dealt most severely with such advocates.

"Even the Man of Nazareth is on our blacklist for having forged a *Scourge of Cords,* tipped over our banking tables, and forcibly driven us out of the Temple.

"You must dispense quickly with your unsound money and adopt a privately-controlled banking system. Great prosperity will be yours and that of your children and all generation, to follow!"

Little did the islanders realize the colossal swindle that was being perpetrated. Blindly, the islanders were falling prey to a system that inevitably would place them, and their unborn children, in bondage to non-producers. . . .

The unit-measurement "dollar"

IN ORDER to set the stage for the advent of the Shylocks from a neighboring island, with their bags of gold, let us give some interim thought to the unit measurement that we call a "dollar." We carefully identified each islander's purchasing power against the island's total goods and services as a "contribution-claim." We wanted it clear that when we came to use the unit-measure "dollar," we could clearly make the distinction between the claim against goods and services and the amount of that claim.

We use "inches" and "miles" to express length. We use "quarts" and "bushels" to express volume. Always we speak of so many inches of **pipe** or so many miles of **road.** In the same practical sense we express the unit measurements of volume as so many quarts of **milk** or so many **bushels** of wheat.

Is it difficult to recognize that logically there must be **goods and services**, or human effort, directly related to "dollars?"

Clearer, and clearer, it will penetrate our thinking the utter fallacy of a nation being restrained in performing work because there is a shortage of "dollars." It would make as much sense to contend that the carpenter couldn't build because he had run out of "inches." Or that the farmer couldn't plant and harvest because he had run out of "bushels." Or that the astronomer must close the doors of his observatory because he had run out of "light-years."

What economic nonsense and economic subterfuge, indeed!

HAVING clarified in our thinking that the "dollar," whether expressed in fractions or multiples, is a unit-measurement, and nothing else, let us arbitrarily set the Gross Domestic Product of our island at $100,000. This would mean, by simple computation, that each of the 100 inhabitants would have in his or her possession an average of $1000 in earned purchasing power.

Isn't it apparent that any arbitrary dollar-value could be placed on the GDP, the totality of goods and services, and then proportionately increase the islander's total "dollar" claims. The direct ratio between all things for purchase, and purchasing power, would still persist?

Witness carefully now what happened. The bankers having succeeded in convincing the islanders of their indispensability got the green light for the accountant-treasurer to provide an extra $10,000 in contribution-claims, not based on any new goods and services, but based on the bags of gold which the bankers had securely placed in an old pirate's cask which they brought with them.

The islanders were much impressed by the promises of the bankers that "prosperity was just around the corner" and that statistics would be forthcoming at the end of each month confirming economic growth.

Ten of the islanders stepped forth immediately, each eager to be a borrower of $1000 in extra contribution-claims, and each anxious to increase his or her purchasing power. Totally unsuspected by the new borrowers was that while the money supply had been increased by 10%, the total goods and services remained the same. In terms of things to be purchased, the island's total purchasing power dwindled to nine-tenths of what it previously had been as the islanders paid back the fictitious "loans" of the private bankers.

The cunning and unscrupulous moneylenders had exploited exactly one-tenth of the labor of all the islanders. Or, more pointedly, they had stolen ten percent of the islander' purchasing power!

WHAT about the ten islanders who went into debt purportedly to acquire additional purchasing power? First, they had to put up their shelters or oxen as collateral. So in fact the "money" that they were given was not based on the banker's gold but on the borrower's own property and working capability. The bankers had taken no risk whatsoever. The borrowers assumed the full risk. If they were unable to pay back the loans, their huts and oxen reverted to the bankers by the way of foreclosures.

Now consider this incredible development: Whereas the loans, or manufactured money, came into circulation as **unearned** dollars, when paid back to the bankers they were received by the debt merchants as **earned** dollars. Isn't it deadly clear that the amount of extra labor that the borrowers had to do in order to pay back the manufactured money, or loans, is the exact amount that was filched from all the islanders in decreased purchasing power?

In short, the islanders lost $10,000 in purchasing power against the goods and services which they had produced and the bankers gained that same amount in their own coffers. And the bankers had not produced one iota of anything in either goods or services!

"Let others work and we'll live off their labor!" became the shibboleth of the bankers as they savored their good fortune. With illusory promises of economic recovery, they would make loans easy to get, and **inflate** the money supply, and in calling in their loans they would **deflate** the money supply. In the process they were not only the beneficiaries of hard-earned dollars but the rate of foreclosures always increased.

Of course, in order to get a loan the borrowers were compelled to pay a tribute to the bankers for the privilege of having their own work potential and assets monetized. The deviltry in the whole procedure was that while the loan could be paid back, since an exact amount of new money had been added to the existing money supply, there had been no extra new money issued to cover the interest. Every loan carried with it unpaid interest in the form of accumulating indebtedness.

The island progressively would be in bondage and beholden to usurers!

Isn't it apparent that in a matter of time, through the process of fictitious loans, all money based on goods and services would be supplanted by the debt-money of the private bankers? Ultimately, they would force the island's government to enact a law that only debt-money was "legal tender" and thereby acceptable in the payment of debts.

And later, as the island-society became more populated and government more structured, taxes could only be paid by the debt-money of the entrenched financiers.

4

The Final Stroke

THERE REMAINED but one final stroke. In their original approach to the islanders the bankers had stressed that those skeptical as to the soundness of the "new money" the bankers provided could have that money redeemed in gold. During the beginning a number of islanders availed themselves of such exchange but the desire for the metal quickly dwindled because the islanders were practical men and women and they could find no particular utilitarian use for the pieces of gold.

The feelings of the banker were quite the opposite. There were other islands to conquer!

Inevitably, all pretenses were removed that the banker's bags of gold served as any backing of the debt-money that was manufactured. Why did the bankers have to make their gold available as security when they had tricked the islanders into putting up their productive capability and assets as the security for the loans the bankers issued?

In fact, so subservient to the bankers were the borrowers that they blindly acquiesced to setting up an Island Depository Insurance Corp., secured by the Islanders, covering any, and all, risks incurred by the bankers.

Since gold no longer was any tangible backing of new "money" that was created, a dictum was decreed that all who possessed gold must return same to the bankers to be redeemed by the islander's own credit. With such confiscated gold back in the hands of the bankers the cycle had been completed. Through sheer deceit, and cunning manipulation, the island's whole money supply had fallen into the hands of the private bankers.

The strategizing debt-merchants had neither parted with anything tangible nor had they produced one solitary item for the island's betterment.

From a system based on worthless bags of gold had been introduced a banking system based entirely on the credit of the people and the resources of the island to be exploited by the private bankers. Whereas the islanders had in the beginning brought "money," their contribution-claims, into circulation without either debt or interest, all the money they now used was in the form of interest-bearing debt and was an obligation against their future earnings and productive potential.

Most seriously, the island's destiny had been placed in the hands of those who were uninterested in the well being of the island but were primarily interested in their own exorbitant profits and expanded assets. . . .

Irrespective of what improvement of tools or methods of production were achieved, the fate of the island, including the well being of all its inhabitants, was foredoomed. Wholesale indebtedness, and periodic panics and depressions, were inevitable.

The islanders had been saddled with a private banking system which not only placed liens against their future earnings in order that they might buy what their labor had already produced but which concentrated the real assets of the island in the hands of those who were non-producers.

Any proposed alternative was squelched as "funny money." The island's Shylocks were sacrosanct and the islanders were shackled into submission by their own ignorance. . . .

To ANYONE who thinks the foregoing is only a hypothetical portrayal of a "money system" and "banking system" that have never existed, and could not exist, is due for a jolting awakening. Not only have we covered broadly, albeit hypothetically, the historical development of banking but we have concluded with the banking system that functions right here in America as these pages are being written.

The only liberty that has been taken was to start off with an adequate and sound money supply, which no nation has ever enjoyed, in order to grasp the insanity and injustice of one manipulated in the interest of only the unscrupulous few.

We have presented the contrast so that it would be readily apparent how ruthless financial strategists can completely subvert the true role of money in an economy. We wanted you to grasp that the only honest and sound money is that which is **directly related to the goods and services that are to be purchased by the very people who made them available.**

We wanted you to get the full impact of how money should automatically come into existence as work is done and no sovereign people should turn their assets and work potential over to debt-merchants to be monetized and then returned in the form of interest-bearing indebtedness.

And finally, we wanted you to appreciate the economic premise that with an honest and workable monetary system, an "accounting banking system," the nation and its citizens could do all the things it wanted to do, and needed to do, with no restraints except for the limits of its own work potential.

Unfettered, the nation's economy would grow and flourish in exact degree to the nation's creative and industrious capabilities.

5

Genesis of Private Banking

THE FIRST and most important observation that must be made is that the whole complex of money, credit and banking is a **creation by human entities**. What must be dispelled from our thinking is that the whole complex had any divine origin and was delivered from on high in the form of some celestial plaques. For good or for evil it has been human hands and human minds that have up the centuries created, promoted and carried out all the aspects of "money and credit" and the role of private banking.

The first enlightenment that must come to the people is that the current private banking system operates on the same fallacious principle as that of its progenitor, the 17the century goldsmith bankers. These were the private bankers who did largely all the banking of Western Europe. It was they who accidentally discovered the ruse of "fractional reserve" lending. Up the centuries it was to serve as the foundation for all private banking.

We get the documented story of the goldsmiths in a publication called "Money Facts, a Supplement to **A Primer on Money,**" which was issued by the Subcommittee on Domestic Finance COMMITTEE ON BANKING AND CURRENCY House of Representatives 88th Congress, 2nd Session, September 21, 1964.

The goldsmiths were the custodians of gold. Those who owned the "precious" metal brought it to them for safe keeping. For each amount of gold deposited the goldsmiths gave the depositor a receipt, which could be presented at any time, and the amount of gold withdrawn. However, owners of the gold found that it was easier to exchange the receipts themselves in conducting their business than to disturb the gold in the vaults of the goldsmiths.

In fact, only a very small percentage ever came to actually redeem their receipts. Consequently the receipts circulated as "money" with no thought, or suspicion, by either buyer or seller, as to lack of any gold backing.

It was this circumstance that led the goldsmith bankers to the cunning and deceptive principle of "fractional reserve" banking. If the larger number of those who possessed the receipts for their deposited gold did not come in and claim their actual gold, what prevented the goldsmiths from loaning out the depositor's gold to others?

In fact, what prevented the goldsmiths from writing out receipts for which no gold even existed? Who would be the wiser as long as they, the goldsmiths, simply maintained in their vaults sufficient gold to meet the claims of the small number who did present their receipts for gold payment?

This is exactly what the goldsmiths proceeded to do. They commenced to manufacture money, issuing receipts that neither had any gold backing nor were backed by either goods or services. They simply used the depositor's gold, not their own, as a fractional reserve against which to create fictitious receipts to be loaned out in the form of interest-bearing debt.

Thus several centuries ago the cunning deceit of fractional reserve lending had its origin. Later it was a brutal concept that was to become the central core of modern banking.

We will cover chronologically how the concept was held in tact and promoted by private international banking entities who ultimately succeeded in foisting the financial octopus on our own unsuspecting nation, its blood-sucking tentacles reaching into every cranny of our lives.

The deception of fractional reserve lending was to have, and has had, catastrophic social and economic impact on all ensuing generations!

~ 6 ~

Money based on debt

THERE is a long evolving history of private banking from the time of the goldsmiths to the Federal Reserve System enacted in the Twentieth Century. It is a consistent history of private bankers using a deceptive form of "reserves" upon which they could increase manifold the money supply by the simple expedient of "manufacturing" money or credit.

Most serious is the fact that all such artificial purchasing power has been put into circulation in the form of debt, obligating the people and their government with perpetual interest-bearing liens against both property and future labor.

The power to expand the money supply automatically carried with it the power to contract the supply. Thus, the power to inflate and deflate the amount of money and credit has consistently given the private bankers the power to destroy the purchasing value of money, affect the price of every product and service, arbitrarily cause depressions at will, burden the nation and the people with mushrooming debt, and progressively concentrate the assets of the nation in the hands of fewer and fewer corporate entities.

For our purposes it is not necessary to make a meticulous coverage of the chronological history of money and banking in this nation. However, we should first note that the framers of the Constitution did specifically intend that the power to control the nation's money should be retained in the hands of the people through the Congress.

Article I, Section 8, Part 5 of the Constitution states, **"Congress shall have the power to coin money, regulate the value thereof, and of foreign coin."** While only the word "coin" was used, because there were no banks of issue at the time, the Supreme Court has upheld the proposition that "whatever power there is over the currency is vested in the Congress."

Within two years after the adoption of the Constitution in 1791, our nation was placed in the clutches of private banking. Alexander Hamilton and the international financiers for whom he was spokesman engineered it. It was accomplished by the enactment of the First National Bank Act, which gave birth, with the very inception of our Republic, to the deceitful philosophy that the only "sound" money is debt-money.

Unsuspectingly, the nation had agreed to turn over to the private bankers the nation's bonds, or credit of the whole citizenry, as a "funding" of the existing debt, then allowing the bankers to issue bank notes on the government bonds. Not only was the power to control the amount of money in circulation placed in private hands but to them was extended the privilege of collecting interest on both the government bonds and the new "money" which they created in the form of loans.

Thus was born the gigantic piece of monetary chicanery that holds sway to the present. Stripped to stark nakedness, it stands exposed as a monument to humankind's naiveté in protecting both its hard work and the products of its labor. And what does such major ignorance encompass?

It encompasses the acceptance that a nation's bonds, secured by the assets of the whole nation,

42

and the citizen's working capacity, are sufficient for the private banks to issue money and make loans, but aren't sufficient for the sovereign people to keep their bonds and put money directly into circulation without incurring any debt or without paying any vampiristic tribute called interest?

Throughout the pages of this book the foregoing paragraph will be central to our most basic understanding relative to the erroneous basis of our money and credit and to the imperative reforms that must take place.

Founding Fathers

OUR FOREBEARS were by no means unmindful of the dangers and burdens of private banking and having its industry and commerce servile to the manipulations of debt-merchants. In vain they pitted their opposition to the private banking interests, which wielded too much power even in the nation's infancy. Thomas Jefferson, author of the Declaration of Independence, the Republic's third President, and the nation's staunchest pleader for a democratic society, expressed this concern in a letter to John Taylor:

> **I believe that banking institutions are more dangerous to our liberties than standing armies. Already they have raised up a money aristocracy that has set the Government at defiance. The issuing power should be taken from the banks and restored to the Government to whom it properly belongs.**

Equally vehement in underscoring the fallacies and dangers inherent in private control of the nation's money supply was President John Adams. Those who have investigated the money question have echoed his reactions, summed up in a letter to Thomas Jefferson, up the entire history of our nation. Terse and to the point, Adams wrote:

> **All the perplexities, confusion and distress in America arise, not from defects in their Constitution or confederation, not from want of honor or virtue, so much as from downright**

ignorance of the nature of coin, credit and circulation.

An ironical twist of events found Jefferson President of the nation at the outbreak of the War of 1812. So dependent was the nation for its money supply on the private bankers that he was compelled to acquiesce to the chartering of the Second Bank of the United States. Twenty years later, President Andrew Jackson vetoed the bill that would have renewed the charter, which expired in 1836.

It is well to note that under President Jackson's tenure the nation was free of all debt. Under no administration, before or after, was the nation to be free of needless interest-bearing indebtedness.

President Jackson, along with Jefferson and Adams, recognized the stupidity of a sovereign nation making itself beholden to private bankers for its supply of money. Why should a nation that had just won its political freedom become subservient to financial despots and thus make a mockery of economic freedom? In his farewell address of March 4, 1837, he minced no words in making this indictment of the privately owned central bank of issue:

> **In the hands of this formidable power, thus organized, was also placed unlimited dominion over the amount of circulating medium, giving it the power to regulate the value of property and the fruits of labor in every quarter of the Union, and to bestow prosperity or bring ruin upon any city or section of the country as might best comport with its own interest or policy. . . .**
>
> **Yet, if you had not conquered, the government would have passed from the hands of the many**

to the hands of the few, and this organized money power from its secret conclave would have dictated the choice of your highest officers and compelled you to make peace or war, as best suited their wishes. The forms of your government might for a time have remained, but its living spirit would have departed from it.

President Andrew Jackson had made a heroic gesture in trying to liberate the nation from the stultifying and exploitive power of private bankers but history must record it only as a gesture. He provided no sound alternative. Government deposits were placed in State banks, which in turn used the public credit in a splurge of reckless lending that led to widespread indebtedness and bank failures. Thus ensued the panic of 1837 with its attendant foreclosures and inflated prices. It was the first of the major economic panics that were to periodically afflict the nation.

~ 8 ~
President Lincoln's
"Greenbacks"

OF ALL the outstanding men who make up the best of American history, Abraham Lincoln perhaps more than anyone understood how wrong it was for any entities other than government to issue the nation's money. He did more than indict the unscrupulous private bankers and challenge their usurped power to place a whole nation in bondage and famish its people. He courageously gave the nation the only honest money its citizens have ever enjoyed.

It was Lincoln who stated:

> **Money is the creature of law, and the creation of the original issue of money should be maintained as an exclusive monopoly of the Nation's Government. . . . The privilege of creating and issuing money is not only the supreme prerogative of the Government; it is the Government's greatest opportunity.**

He took positive steps to fulfill his conviction. . . .

During the early years of the Civil War, Lincoln through the Congress succeeded in issuing four hundred and fifty million dollars ($450,000,000) of United States legal tender notes without one cent of either indebtedness or interest incurred by the nation. Such Constitutional money was called "greenbacks" and was secured by the assets of the entire United States.

Why need a great and sovereign nation turn its credit over to private bankers to be rented back in the form of interest-bearing indebtedness? Couldn't all of the nation's money supply, geared to its economic need, be brought into existence without saddling the nation, and its citizens, with liabilities for the use of its own credit and assets? The answer is emphatically affirmative, but the private usurers and bondsmen had no disposition to tolerate a circumvention of their merry game of siphoning off the wealth of the nation.

There is ample evidence leading one to believe that Lincoln signed his own death warrant when he took the first bold step to abolish financial servitude. Whereas his Emancipation Proclamation decreed the abolition of physical slavery for a large segment of the population, his issuance of "greenbacks" decreed the abolition of economic slavery for every man, woman and child in the nation. But ruthless and avaricious financiers were not to be thwarted in their systematic sacking of the virgin territory and untapped resources of the new nation.

Not able to stop the issuance of nearly half a billion dollars in Constitutional and sound money, the banking syndicate was successful in placing a limitation on the "greenbacks" themselves. Thus, these notes bore upon their face the following: *"This note is a legal tender at its face value for all debts, **except duties on imports and interest on the public debt.**"*

It was this exception clause which forced government and importers to kowtow to private bankers and ultimately depreciated the "greenbacks". In 1879, after all the depreciated greenbacks had been bought up by financial speculators, Congress was induced to pass a law that all the notes issued during the Civil War were to be redeemed at face value in gold.

It was another triumph for the nation's debt-merchants.

Lincoln's efforts not only to unmask but also to destroy the gargantuan deceit of private banking were to no avail. Nevertheless he had made a valorous attempt to erase both over-burdening debt and pyramiding interest from the economic lives of all the generations to follow.

He recognized that debt and interest are cancerous growths which devalue human toil, stifle progress and have no place in an equitable and unfettered economy.

If Lincoln had been successful in introducing the nation to a sound and honest money supply, the other built-in evils of predatory capitalism would have crumbled. Over a century and a half of wholesale foreclosures, hardships, anguish and periodic economic breakdowns would have been precluded.

Labor is Superior to Capital

THE depth and far-reaching logic of Lincoln's thinking relative to other elements connected to finance is borne out by his utterances regarding labor and capital. In a speech before the Wisconsin State Agricultural Fair on September 30, 1859 he stated:

> The world is agreed that labor is the source from which human wants are mainly supplied. There is no dispute upon this point. From this point, however, men immediately diverge. Much disputation is maintained as to the best way of

applying and controlling this labor element. By some it is assumed that labor is available only in connection with capital. . . that nobody labors, unless somebody else, owning capital, somehow, by the use of that capital induces him to do it. . .

But another class of reasoners hold the opinion that there is no such relation between capital and labor as assumed; and that there is no such thing as a freeman being fatally fixed for life in the condition of a hired laborer; that both these assumptions are false, and all inferences from them groundless. They hold that labor is prior to, and independent of capital; that in fact, capital is the fruit of labor, and could never have existed if labor had not first existed; that labor can exist without capital, but that capital could never have existence without labor.

Hence, they hold that labor is <u>the superior, greatly the superior, of capital</u>.

These two paragraphs, particularly the second, should be read and re-read by every person who is seriously interested in bringing about a society that is not beholden to the restraints of an archaic and falsely-premised private banking system. The intrinsic element in providing all needs of the society must be the ingenuity and labor of its members.

Capital can only, and should only, come into existence as it directly relates to human effort. As Lincoln stated, "<u>labor is the superior, greatly *superior, of capital*</u>."

~ 9 ~

Usurers move with a vengeance

HOLDING over $2,600,000,000 of interest-bearing bonds, which the government had been forced to sell to the banks to underwrite the costs of the Civil War, the bankers compelled the passage of the National Bank Act. The Congress was helpless to offer any opposition.

Under the newly enacted law, the national banks were granted the privilege of depositing their purchased bonds with the Treasurer of the United States and then to issue up to 90% of those bonds in bank notes to private borrowers. Thus on precisely the same money, they collected 6% interest on the bonds themselves and a similar interest, usually more, on the private bank notes they "manufactured."

From the time of the Civil War up to the present there is a perpetual history of how private banks and their syndicates have inveigled out of Congress privileged and unconstitutional legislation giving them despotic control of the nation's money supply. No small part of their intrigue involved their garnering of the gold and getting Congressional sanction that any money issued by the government must be redeemed in the precious metal owned by the private banks.

Thus, they could prevent the United States government from interfering with the banker's exclusive monopoly.

Throughout the monetary history of this nation the private banks have promoted the calculated deception that gold is the only sound basis for a nation's money supply. The fact that such basis permitted them to

51

control the money supply simply by cornering the gold supply was carefully kept from the people.

What should have registered with the people with shocking impact is this challenging question: If the whole purpose of a money supply is to facilitate the exchange of goods and services, and to provide for productive expansion, why then shouldn't all money be related directly to those goods, services and production?

Rational thinking should have dictated that a nation's progress and well being should be directly related to its natural resources, human energy, technology and the ingenuity of the whole nation instead of being beholden to some mystic quality of a metal!

Not having any understanding of how his money and loans were created, or more importantly, how they were both arbitrarily determined, the unsuspecting citizen accepted the promoted fiction that both his cash and loans were backed by gold. While it is true that prior to 1934 the legal promise existed to convert both currency and bank deposits into gold, no such amount of gold actually existed.

For example, when the Federal Reserve was organized in 1914, the total deposits and currency in circulation amounted to 20 billion dollars, but there was only 1.6 billion dollars of monetary gold in the country. In other words, the amount of money in circulation was 12 times the amount of gold. According to figures from the House Committee on Banking and Currency, a similar proportion held true fifty years later in 1963. At that time the money supply, both cash and checks, totaled 157.4 billion dollars and the Treasury's gold was only 15.6 billion dollars.

However, citing these figures is begging the point. In 1934, the private banking institutions succeeded in pushing through a law that not only made it illegal to possess gold but no American citizen could demand gold in exchange for his dollars. As usual, of course, there was an exception for non-Americans. Foreigners holding American credit could through their banks demand and have their dollars converted into gold bullion.

From a private banking system based on useless bags of gold, we have come supinely to accept an **entire money supply based on debt, interest-bearing debt.**

Not one person in a thousand, more likely, not one in a hundred thousand, recognizes the hoax that private bankers have perpetrated on the nation, its citizens and their government. Unsuspectingly, the people and their government have turned over their assets and their earning capacity to the private banks to be monetized and lent back to them in the form of interest-bearing indebtedness.

Slowly but surely more and more people are beginning to recognize the fallacious gimmick of fractional reserve lending which permits the private banks to grant loans, and bear in mind that it is the people's assets or working capacity that makes the loans good, upwards of ten times the reserves of the bank itself. All such loans are nothing but the **manufacture** of checkbook credit.

Every time a loan is made this is money that had no existence prior to its creation by the private banks.

The arbitrary power to expand and contract the money supply, by the making of loans or calling them in, has placed in the hands of the private bankers the power not only to change the purchasing worth of the dollar but has given them the power literally to control the amount of work the nation can perform.

The nation's entire working capacity and its well-being has been made beholden to the whim and greed of nonproducers.

~ 10 ~

"On a cross of gold"

FROM THE TIME of the Civil War and through the balance of the Nineteenth Century courageous representatives of the people fought a real struggle to establish "silver" as a backing of the nation's money supply. The private banks were frantically determined to deny the people this approach, which would have increased the taxpayer's purchasing power and the nation's ability to fund needed enterprises. They did every thing they could in manipulating Congress to "de-monitize silver".

What was their motivation? The private bankers exclusively controlled the amount of gold and to the extent another metal was introduced as a backing of the nation's money supply they would lose their ironclad economic power over the working capability of the nation. They had no disposition to let anyone interfere with their monopolistic control of the nation's monetary needs.

One of the nation's most insightful and courageous fighters for an honest money system was Jerry Voorhis, Congressman from California for five terms. His book, **Out of Debt, Out of Danger** (Devin-Adair, New York, 1943) is must reading for anyone who wants to understand the unconstitutional role of private banking and the economic suffering that it has imposed on the American people.

Congressman Voorhis covers in considerable detail the multiple billions of dollars that were garnered by the banks by their manipulating the Congress to demonetize silver. He gives us a clear picture of the struggle involved. We quote from his book on page 48:

> In any case, the national bankers (who were of course very far from being really "national") were afraid of silver because an abundant coinage of silver by the government would to a certain extent have broken their monopoly of the money supply of this young and expanding nation. And in any period of expanding wealth production all anyone with money or the power to create money has to do is to sit on his money or his power and let the rest of the nation, by its labors, increase the purchasing power of his interest income.
>
> For if money in circulation increases less rapidly than the production of real wealth, there is that much more real wealth per dollar which means that every dollar will buy and have command over that much more real goods, services and wealth.
>
> No wonder "Wall Street" and all it has stood for grew and flourished in this period of the National Bank Act, and gold!

A bill was passed through Congress in 1873 without debate or explanation. It was the regular coinage bill for that year. Members of both the House and Senate were kept in ignorance of the fact that the bill made **no mention of the coinage of any silver**. When they protested, it was too late. Silver had been demonitized and the supply of money sharply reduced.

Another victory for the private bankers, which we have alluded to earlier in the book, was a law passed in 1879 providing that all of the United States notes (Greenbacks) issued during the Civil War *should be redeemable at face value in gold.* Since the notes had depreciated sharply in value, due to the limitations that the private banks had succeeded in placing on them, the nation's speculators had garnered the larger number.

It was another financial victory for the bankers and helped perpetuate their mastery over gold!

Voorhis underscores the fundamental thinking of President Lincoln with these words:

> **Abraham Lincoln saw with his clear simple vision that it was wrong for anyone except government to exercise the power of monetary issue. He saw that neither gold nor silver nor both of them together could ever supply an adequate amount of money for modern business.**
>
> **He saw that if this was attempted it would be easy for a few men by controlling the stocks of the precious metals to decide precisely how much money the nation should or should not have and to bring about with deliberate intent sharp rises and falls in the money value of every bit of real wealth and every hour of labor in America.**
>
> **Lincoln understood the basic injustice of privately manufactured money and perceived that whenever the government borrowed such privately manufactured money it imposed upon its people debt-that-ought-not-to-be-debt, the interest upon which was in the nature of a pure tribute devised by clever bookkeepers.**

In his book Voorhis raises a serious speculation that has surfaced over the years as to the real motivation for Lincoln's assassination. What role might the financial interests, directly and indirectly, have had in

57

causing the demise of their primary antagonist? Wasn't there real concern from their standpoint that unmasking of the whole spectrum of debt-money based on mythical metals would be fatal to their control of the nation's economic bloodstream?

We will never know the real motivation behind Lincoln's assassination. But one thing is certain: The destiny of the United States would have been radically different if the people had adopted Lincoln's major break-through in giving the nation a debt-free and interest-free money system.

In summary, Voorhis was concerned that there not be a misconception relative to silver. He stated:

> "Free silver" was important. It was important because had there been "free and unlimited coinage of silver at the rate of 16:1 to gold," this would have given the country at least one kind of money that did not have to be redeemed in gold and would thus not have been subject to the power of Wall Street to cause inflation and deflation for its own benefit.

> But "free silver" would not have given the nation a scientific or right monetary system. Indeed it is doubtful whether in the long run, had it been adopted, it would have turned out any better than the Gold Standard. For like gold, silver is a single commodity subject to be bought and sold and hence hoarded and released from hoarding.

> And like gold, there is absolutely no reason under Heaven why anyone in his right mind should expect that the production of silver mines will over any period increase in the same, or anywhere near the same, ratio as the

production of real wealth, i.e., of the goods and services the people need and use.

Therefore, the same basic and absolutely indisputable arguments, which apply against tying the whole economic system of a nation and the destiny and happiness of its people to one commodity, apply alike against both silver and gold.

In this chapter we have not dealt with the economic devastation that took place from the time of the Civil War up to the end of the 19th Century due to the private control of the nation's monetary needs. Panics were persistent throughout that period with tragic loss through foreclosures of farm and business, millions jobless, and pervading want in the midst of plenty.

William Jennings Bryan, a candidate for the presidency of the United States, in a speech in 1896, highlighted the cause of the suffering the people had endured when he exclaimed that they had been "crucified on a Cross of Gold."

In the next chapter we will commence to deal with the 20th Century when the nation had foisted on itself "The Fed," the nation's central banking system.

~11~

"The Fed"

WE WILL NOW **focus** directly on "The Fed" and deal in a documented way with the central banking system that has held full sway up to the present time since the Federal Reserve Act was passed by the United States Congress on December 28, 1913. We first want to deal with the worldly financial environment that set the stage for the first steps toward the passage of the Act.

To appreciate its passage we first have to give thought to the background of international banking. We have to understand the centuries of cunning maneuvering to establish a world network of central banking systems.

There is need to go back to the Goldsmith Bankers, who we have already introduced, and bring in the worldly role of the **Rothschilds**, the international banking family whose reign in finance began at the end of the eighteenth century and whose influence has endured to the present time.

We are fortunate to have in our hands a book called **The Rothschilds: A Family Portrait** (Curtis Atheneum, New York, 1962), written by Frederick Morton who had personal contact with members of the Rothschild family in writing his book.

No one has written a coverage so comprehensive and so candid as Mr. Morton has done.. On the inside cover we read: "The Rothschilds' story begins at the end of the eighteenth century with Mayer Amschel Rothschild, a Frankfurt money changer. From a cramped house in Frankfurt's Jew Street he built a financial empire that his five sons carried to five European capitals and finally to world-wide power."

With much detail and character portrayal the author covers the financial triumphs of the five sons and how they became "bankers to empires, creators of the modern concept of international finance, builders of the European continent's first railroads." The author covers two centuries of the financial power and political intrigue exercised by the Rothschild dynasty. There were none who could stay their hand.

On page 13 and 14 we read:

> "Yet here, in a cramped ghetto dwelling, the great Pauillac wedding had its roots. Here, with a yellow star pinned to his caftan, Mayer Amschel Rotschild kept a small store two centuries ago, and married Gutele Schnapper, and raised with her those five incredible sons who conquered the world more thoroughly, more cunningly and much more lastingly than all the Caesars before or all the Hitlers after them." (emphasis by author)

What concerns us is that the central banking systems that they so successfully set up throughout Europe was the same devilish private banking system that they had slated for America. It was their projected goal to realize a private banking system of interest-bearing debt in every major country in the world. Undeveloped countries could be exploited indirectly.

The two-century financial onslaught of the Rothschilds in Europe and on other continents was prelude to an inevitable and contemplated ownership and control of the United States credit and monetary needs. We have already referred to the role of the International

Bankers at the very inception of the nation when they compelled the Colonists to set up the First National Bank.

During the latter half of the 19th century we covered how they were able to thwart Lincoln's introduction of the "Greenbacks" honest funding and how they succeeded in the enacting of the Second National Bank Act. Most importantly, we demonstrated their manipulative role in the whole issue of gold and silver as deceptive backing of the nation's credit and money.

The beginning of the 20th century found the nation in the throes of the 1907 Panic. The stringent economic conditions, which the banks had brought about, ironically, were the ideal circumstances leading to the "mother of all take-overs". A century of repeated depressions and panics had set the stage for the enactment of a central banking system patterned after what the Rothschilds had achieved throughout Europe.

The person to spearhead the effort was the offspring of a prominent German banking family. He was Paul Warburg, son of the banking family of M.M. Warburg & Company.

Warburg Spearheads Efforts

WE GET personal history of Paul Warburg from **The Region**, publication of the Minneapolis Federal Reserve Bank issued in May 1989. The article is entitled "Paul Warburg's Crusade to Establish a Central Bank in the United States." It is well to know some of his background in view of the critical role he played in achieving the passing of the Federal Reserve Act on December 28, 1913.

We quote from the article in "The Region":

Paul Warburg was born in Hamburg in 1868. The offspring of a prominent German banking family, he had been trained in banking in the European capitals. After attending the university at age 18 he began his career in London where for two years he worked for a banking and discounting firm, followed by a short stint with a London stockbroker.

After that he moved to France and gained additional experience at the Russian bank for foreign trade, which had an agency in Paris. He then traveled to India, China and Japan before returning to Hamburg to become a partner in M. M. Warburg & Co., the family banking firm.

Warburg's father had fully expected that Paul would take charge of his family's business along with his brothers Aby and Max, but in 1895 Warburg married an American citizen, Nina Loeb, an accomplished violinist, and began to live part of the year in New York. Six years later, at age 34, he left Germany, took up permanent residency in the United States, and accepted a position as a partner at his father-in-laws firm, Kuhn, Loeb and Co., one of Wall Street's most important banks.

An excerpt from Paul M. Warburg's own writings, "The Federal Reserve System, Its Origin and Growth," indicate that he did a great deal to bring about the passage of the Federal Reserve Act in its final form:

I do not claim to have originated any new banking principle; but from my arrival in America I have been impelled to urge the adoption of the fundamental principles upon which, under varying forms, were based the practices of every industrially advanced country except the United States.

It was owing to the interest I had shown in banking reform that, when the Aldrich Banking & Currency Committee was appointed, I was invited to assist it in formulating a plan providing for the creation of a Central Reserve Association with regional branches.

It should be mentioned that Warburg's career didn't end with passage of the Federal Reserve Act. In a sense, the close of this chapter marked the beginning of his next important role as a central banker. As an officer of his father-in-law's international bank, Kuhn, Loeb and Company, he wielded tremendous influence on the future of the System he worked so hard to establish.

Because of his ties to, and knowledge of, international finances, he was invaluable to the whole network of central banking systems throughout the world. President Wilson appointed him to become a member of the first Federal Reserve Board and he served as both sustainer and defender of the interests of private banking.

"Money Creators"

FOR THOSE seriously interested in the historical evolution of private banking in the United States, a book called **Money Creators**, researched and put into print by Gertrude M. Coogan, is essential to have in one's library. What makes this book so important and credible is that the introduction was written by Senator Robert L. Owen who was Chairman of the Committee on Banking and Currency of the United States Senate in which he served for 18 years.

Along with Hon. Carter Glass and Senator Aldrich, Senator Owen was a sponsor of the legislation that led finally to the enactment of the Federal Reserve Act. However, during the discussions and deliberations, he was much disenchanted with the provisions that were eliminated. At a later date is felt that he and the American people had been betrayed.

In the book **Money Creators** we find especially pertinent references to Paul Warburg and his role in bringing about the Federal Reserve System. Edwin Seligman in his introductory remarks of August 1914 to Paul Warburg's book "Essays on Banking Reform in the United States" stated:

> **"For it may be stated without fear of contradiction that in its fundamental features the Federal Reserve Act is the work of Mr. Warburg more than any other man in the country."**

The book further states, "Mr. Warburg did not tell the American people that the privately owned Central Banks of England, France and Germany were the result of long years of conniving on the part of international money controllers."

Miss Coogan makes certain succinct conclusions as to the flaws and evil inherent in the Federal Reserve Act that was passed. She stated:

> **The Federal Reserve Act as passed and later amended and administered was a serious mistake. It turned over to the international bankers complete control over the banking system of this country, and hence, over all business. It was the central control of the credit in the entire nation that resulted in the rapid**

concentration of ownership in all lines of business.

The system is enslaving the unfortunate individuals who are forced to earn their living by being part of an organization operated from a distant city. These slaves should be liberated for better positions, impossible under our present money system.

She then cites a development that we of this day can so clearly relate to respecting corporate concentration and ownership of the nation's wealth and work capability. She was prophetic in her conclusion:

Had the money control of this country never been centralized, and had it not been turned over to exploiters, the terrible concentration of control and ownership of wealth could never have been brought about . . . There is absolutely no hope of the United States restoring this country to a condition wherein worthy Americans can earn a living in permanent security unless the power to create money is restored where it belongs—to the Congress of the United States.

Finally, she offers this admonition:

No individual should ever be allowed the privilege and power of creating and recalling money at will. An individual who counterfeited a few dimes would be sent to the penitentiary and rightfully so, but what about bankers who are given unconstitutional powers to create vast sums of their privately created money and lend it at interest to the United States Government itself?

Could anything be more stupid than to permit such a system to continue?

We would highly recommend Miss Coogan's book **Money Creators** (Omini Publications, Hawthorne CA, 1935) as the most encompassing coverage of the evolving history of private banking since the very inception of our nation. As we have already mentioned the credibility of her work is indisputably vouched for by the introduction to her book by Senator Robert L. Owen who was Chairman of the Committee on Banking and Currency of the United States Senate.

We now want to focus on a member of the United States Congress who deserves center stage in his battle with the "Money Trust" that was hell-bent in enacting the Federal Reserve Act.

Father of
"The Lone Eagle"

THROUGHOUT the nation there were many men and women who recognized the evils and predatory aspects of private banking. However, no one waged as relentless and courageous battle against the powerful "Money Trust" and the passage of the Federal Reserve Act in 1913 as Representative Charles A. Lindbergh.

From 1908 to 1918 he was a U. S. Representative from Minnesota and he not only waged a fight against the powerful banking interests in the Halls of State but in the writing of several books and in his campaigning for governor of Minnesota. Up the years the nation's capitalists whose exploitive existence was dependent on the populace ignorance have suppressed his books.

Representative Lindbergh's son, Charles A. Lindbergh, Jr. was, of course, America's famed hero, "The Lone Eagle," who was the first person to make a solo trans-Atlantic flight (1927), which gave him an heroic fame that resounded up the balance of the 20th Century and into the 21st. Father and son had a very close relationship and while their challenges in life were quite different, their steadfastness in pursuit of goals bears out an inherent genetic drive they both shared.

Every person who is concerned as to how our financial-economic system is flawed and wrongly structured, and how powerful predatory forces have risen in our midst in consequence, should read Lindbergh's books and speeches delivered on the floor of Congress.

Covering the dire conditions that existed prior to the calculated thrust by Warburg and others to achieve passage of the Federal Reserve Act, Lindbergh had this to say in his book **Banking and Currency and the Money Trust:**

> Most men are in a condition of poverty now. Also, we absolutely know that the trusts, as a result of the centralizing of the control of the industrial agencies and material resources, operated in connection with their juggling of credits and money, have made us dependent upon the trusts for employment.
>
> This is the industrial slavery that the capitalistic interests prefer to chattel slavery. If we were chattel slaves, they would have to care for us in sickness and old age, whereas now they are not concerned with us except for the time during which we work for them.
>
> Knowing these facts, will the people continue to remain in such a state of bondage? Certainly not! The trusts have taught us the principle of combination. If it is good and profitable for the trusts, it is good and profitable for the people. It would be better to have <u>one great trust created by all of the people for their common benefit</u> than to have our actions controlled by several trusts operated for the individual benefit of a few persons.

Lindbergh was well aware that inevitably there had to be a day of reckoning when the "Money Trust" must give way to a "Public Trust" that included all the people.

Lindbergh's battle in the Congress reflects the persistence he demonstrated in opposing the "Aldrich

Monetary Commission" whose hearings led to the enactment of the Federal Reserve Act. We quote from a book called **The Story of Money** by Olive Cushing Dwinell who characterizes her book as a "brief history of our money as it is revealed from records of unquestioned authority." We quote from her book on page 189:

> **Representative Lindbergh from Minnesota, father of the world famous flier, was one of the most consistent and ardent supporters of government issued money during his ten years in the House of Representatives. He is said to be the only man known in Congress who read the entire 20 volumes of the Aldrich Monetary Commission. Such a Niagara of words poured over a Congressman on one bill raises the suspicion among reasonable people that those interests responsible for it are purposely making it impossible for Congressmen to digest it.**

Lindbergh had grave concern about the Aldrich Banking and Currency Plan as to the power that would be vested in the large banks. He referred to it as a monstrous scheme of concentrated power and the country would be at the mercy of the Money Trust. He stated:

> **It would admit of no membership except banks and trust companies, and exclude the smaller ones of these. The rest of the world would not only be excluded from holding stock, but by the nature of the association, powers and relations of finance to commerce, it would dictate the terms on which business should be done.**
>
> **With that power centered in the great city banks and these banks controlled by the trusts and money powers, the politics as well as the**

business of the country would be under its dictation.

The government prosecuted other trusts, but supports the money trust. I have been waiting patiently for several years for an opportunity to expose the false money standard, and to show that <u>the greatest of all favoritism is that extended by the government to the money trust.</u> (emphasis by the author)

From his book **Your Country at War**, written in 1917, we glean Lindbergh's clear thinking about the broad economic condition that existed with the nation in the clutches of private banking. He underscores the contradiction of the technological ability to provide a good life for everyone while at the same time there exists extreme misery and poverty. On page 203, Lindbergh wrote:

It is unfortunate, but it is nevertheless true, that as mechanical devices have been invented, that as new ways have been discovered and applied to multiply the products of human energy, that while all these have taken place to make this period the most scientific as well as the most productive in all the history of the world, the masses nevertheless have become more dependent, and exist now as industrial slaves.

Tragically, this contradiction has persisted to this day as we enter the 21st Century; only the lines of demarcation between those who control the means of production and the disadvantaged are more clearly drawn. Increased corporate ownership and control of the nation's work capability, the inability of private capitalism to accommodate advancing technology, the "downsizing" of the best paying jobs, mushrooming indebtedness---all contribute to a land of "haves" and "have-nots".

Lindbergh recognized that our economic and financial system was flawed and that the biggest omission of the workers, consumers and taxpayers was their failure to demand equity in the technology, machinery and plants that their sweat and blood, and tax dollars, made possible.

As already emphasized, he was well aware that inevitably the "Money Trust" must give way to a "Public Trust" that included all the people.

We now want to give thought to studies by Congressional Committees during the last half of the 20th Century which establish overwhelmingly the control of the Federal Reserve System by the most powerful corporate entities in the nation.

~ 13 ~
Corporate influence

HENRY S. REUSS, Chairman of the *Banking, Currency and Housing Committee of the U. S. House of Representatives* had this to say in his opening remarks of the Study, August, 1976, entitled: FEDERAL RESERVE DIRECTORS: A STUDY OF CORPORATE AND BANKING INFLUENCE:

> **As the study makes clear, it is difficult to imagine a more narrowly based board of directors for a public agency than has been gathered together for the twelve banks of the Federal Reserve System.**

Only two segments of American society, banking and big business, have any substantial representation on the boards, and often even these become merged through interlocking directorates.

What makes this study so pertinent to the whole area of interlocking directorates is that it so clearly dispels the promoted myth that the Federal Reserve System is independent of corporate interests. At the outset Chairman Henry Reuss (D. Wisconsin) stated:

> **The big business and banking dominance of the Federal Reserve System cited in this report can be traced, in part, to the original Federal Reserve Act, which gave member commercial banks the right to select two-thirds of the directors of each district bank.**

> **They are the directors, for example, who initially select the presidents of the 12 district banks who serve on the Open Market Committee**

determining the nation's money supply and the level of economic activity.

Chairman Reuss than got specific as to who are the directors of the 12 Federal Reserve district banks and to what powerful groups they are beholden, and who influences their decisions.

> The selection of these public officials, with such broad and essential policy-making powers, should not be in the hands of boards of directors selected and dominated by private corporate interests. . . . In fact, many directors of the Federal Reserve District banks are members of the U. S. Chamber of Commerce, the National Association of Manufacturers, groups with long histories of opposition to organized labor.

> . . . Small farmers are absent. Small business is barely visible. No women appear on the district boards and only six among the branches. System-wide, including district and branch boards, only thirteen members from minority groups appear.

The Study brought out the nature of "The Club System" in which there are consistent and pervasive ties of Corporate America with the Federal Reserve System. Here is how it was reported along with many pages of confirmation:

> While Corporate America has wide representation—through director interlocks—with all twelve banks in the Federal Reserve System, analysis of each district bank and crosschecking one district bank with the others reveals not only the narrow pool of talent but the "club" nature of the system.

This "club" approach leads the Federal Reserve to consistently dip into the same pools—the same companies, the same universities, the same bank holding companies—to fill directorships. This is particularly true in connection with those positions where the Board of Governors and/or the district banks have the right of appointment—the Class C directorships on the district boards and the various branch director positions.

Under the heading "The Public Relations-Lobbying Factor" the Study had this to say:

At the national level, some of the activities of the Federal Reserve directors are masked behind their corporate shields, and it is difficult to distinguish the lobbying generated by the Federal Reserve banks from that of the corporate banking lobby.

When the lobbying pressure mounted against the new audit proposal in 1975, a study was conducted by the late Wright Patman, which revealed the close relationship between the private lobbying organization and our supposedly "public" Federal Reserve System.

The Study showed that 45 of the 164 member corporations are represented on the board of directors of the Federal Reserve district banks and branches. Eighteen of the corporations represented on the 40-member policy committee of the Business Roundtable are also represented on the boards of the district banks and branches.

Another big business organization, the United States Chamber of Commerce, also has substantial interlocks with the Federal Reserve. The Chamber, which often lobbies on banking

and Federal Reserve legislation, has a 52-member policy committee on banking, monetary and fiscal affairs. Thirty-one of these members are officers or directors of banks and 8 have director interlocks with the Federal Reserve System.

Certainly, there can be no dispute that the whole Federal Reserve System, including its 12 district banks, its branches, its member banks, and the Federal Reserve Board, is an exclusive banker's fraternity operating in the interest **of** bankers, **for** bankers and **by** bankers, all to the public's detriment.

During the 1980s and the 1990s, and into the 21st Century, there has been a field day for the nation's largest corporations, both financial and commercial, in creating larger and more monopolistic giants. A mania of mergers has flagrantly circumvented the major anti-trust laws. The whole tragic development, with greedy CEO abuses, "cooking" of books, destruction of pension funds and loss of millions of jobs through "downsizing" have all taken place under the protective umbrella of the Federal Reserve System.

We have been witness to a period of callous disregard of the public interest and a demonstration of the **arrogance of power** when perpetrators are not made legally accountable.

Bankers Testify Under Oath

TO THOSE WHO are unacquainted with the ramifications of banking and money control, it may be a surprise to learn that countless books have been written on the subject up the centuries. The incredible circumstance is that so much knowledge could have existed without sufficient people rising in enlightened protest to demand monetary reform. (A number of books on the subject are listed in the bibliography).

While there has been no dearth of information available on either the forces or personalities behind private banking or the diabolical power that they have exercised, and do exercise, the real difficulty has been in getting large enough numbers of people to accept the truth of the allegations.

One of the chief obstacles has been that most of the writings on, and analyses of, money and banking have embodied very little direct testimony by bankers themselves. Thus, the accused could continue to promote the doubt in the reader's mind that the accusers were presenting an erroneous case. Like the yokel who saw a giraffe for the first time, the reader was conditioned to react, "There just ain't such an animal!"

However, a most fortunate development came to pass. It was to mark the end of any deceptive counteraction that those who were endeavoring to awaken the people to the iniquitous machinations of private banking were subverters of the public trust and advocates of "funny money" schemes. Out of the mouths of the bankers themselves, under oath, was to come the whole story of the workings of their own nefarious system.

For the whole year of 1964, spring, summer and fall, a committee of the United States Congress conducted extensive hearings into the operations of the Federal Reserve System. No aspect or ramification of the 50-year existence of the nation's private banking system was left unscrutinized.

It was the first time in the history of the nation that a duly constituted Committee of Congress had so penetratingly and thoroughly investigated the issuance and control of our whole money supply.

The man who spearheaded the investigation was Representative Wright Patman of Texas who was the **Chairman of the House Committee on Banking and Currency**, and was also the **Chairman of the Subcommittee on House and Finance,** which was responsible for the hearings.

It should be noted that Representative Patman had been for 40 years one of the nation's most knowledgeable and forceful critics of the private controlled Federal Reserve System. He had authored many resolutions during his lifetime for checking the System's operations and he stressed consistently that under the Constitution it is the right and duty of Congress to create and control the money supply of the nation.

The hearings are too voluminous for the average person to read en toto. However, for the scholar there is now available an historic and documented record of how private banking operates and how the nation's whole economy is despotically influenced by its actions.

Not only were all the executives of the Federal Reserve System itself, the 12 presidents of the Federal Reserve Banks and the seven members of the Federal Reserve Board, meticulously interrogated but included as well were the Secretary of the Treasury, officials of the General Accounting Office, representatives of the American Bankers Association, the Independent Bankers Association and representatives of the commercial banks.

Included also were dozens of experts representing a wide range of testimony. Among them were the President of the Cooperative League, the research director of the AFL-CIO, past advisors to President Truman and Kennedy, and a number of outstanding authorities on law, political economy and public administration. In addition, many statements and exhibits were all made part of the hearings.

The three volumes entitled **"The Federal Reserve System After Fifty Years"** fill over 2260 pages of hearings. Corollary volumes make a stack of priceless documentation over a foot high.

At the conclusion of the hearings, the majority of members of the Subcommittee made specific recommendations, and later introduced bills, for the express purpose of reversing high interest rates and tight money, and curbing the exorbitant power of the private banks which control the Federal Reserve System. All efforts were to no avail.

The extent to which banking lobbies will go was graphically borne out by the attempted bribe of Representative Gonzales, a member of the Subcommittee from Texas. He testified that he had been offered a position on the Board of Directors of a bank coupled with a stock gift. Such barefaced attempts at bribery have been a common practice over the years.

At a later time Representative Gonzales became **Chairman of the House Committee on Banking and Currency** and admirably filled the shoes of Chairman Patman who preceded him.

Our next chapter will introduce the 144-page booklet called "A Primer on Money" which was put together for the Subcommittee. It not only reflects the basic information gained from the 3-volume hearings entitled "The Federal Reserve After Fifty Years" but explains in simplified language how our private banking system operates.

~ 15 ~
"A Primer on Money"

IN A "LETTER OF TRANSMITTAL" Chairman Wright Patman had this to say to members of the **Subcommittee on Domestic Finance:**

> Transmitted herewith for the use of the Sub-Committee on Domestic Finance of the Banking and Currency committee is "A Primer on Money," which explains in simple, everyday language how our monetary system works and indicates where it needs reform.
>
> For a great many years I have been concerned with the need for more popular information on this very important subject, and, as time permitted over the years, this publication emerged from the notes, which I have kept.
>
> While responsible for preparation of this "primer," I am indebted to many colleagues throughout the years and to members of the Banking and Currency Committee staff for their valuable suggestions. At the same time, I wish to express my gratitude to a great scholar, Dr. Seymour Harris of Harvard University, whose encouraging sentiments appear immediately following.
>
> It is a source of deep gratification to me that the majority members of the subcommittee voted unanimously to have the "primer" printed as a subcommittee print, the number representing a majority of the committee.

Before dealing with the substance of the release, it is most fitting to cite a few paragraphs of Dr. Seymour E.

Harris, Littauer professor of political economy, Harvard University (emeritus). He is singularly qualified to make an assessment of Congressman Patman and his work. These are his introductory remarks:

> Congressman Patman's "A Primer on Money" is a reminder of the unique service, which the Congressman has given the American people in the last 40 years. No one has defended the interest of the people more vigorously, more persistently, and more courageously against those who have assumed the responsibility of determining how much money there is to be, at what price, and who is to get it.
>
> In the primer one will find a thoughtful elementary discussion of monetary policy and the relation of monetary to other facets of policy. But the primer contains, also, the Congressman's views on the most controversial issues of the day.
>
> Here, for example, one will find a view well defended and needing to be presented, that the Constitution gives to the Congress, and not to the Federal Reserve or the commercial banks, the power to create money and determine the value thereof. There is more than an implication that the Congress has surrendered its prerogative too easily.

"A Primer on Money" is 144 pages long with a most comprehensive index covering every aspect of the Federal Reserve System. The format of the presentation is in the form of questions and the answers are succinct and constructed for the enlightenment of ordinary citizens. Let us choose the most pertinent questions with answers:

Who should have the power to create money?

<u>Answer</u> The power to create money is an inherent power of Government. As President Lincoln said

> **"The privilege of creating and issuing money is not only the supreme prerogative of the Government, it is the Government's greatest opportunity."**

During the past several centuries, various governments in the Western World have, at various times, delegated the money-creating power to private groups or had this power taken from them by default. In these situations, control of the Nation's affairs has been not so much in the hands of the official head of state, but in the hands of the private groups controlling the money system. A famous British banker once summed up the matter this way:

> **They who control the credit of the nation direct the policy of governments, and hold in their hands the destiny of the people."** (Reginald McKenna, Chancellor of the Exchequer in Britain during the World War I period.)

As we look over human history, we find that the tribal chief, the king, the pharaoh, or the emperor has usually had direct or indirect control of the society's money. In the modern, constitutional governments, one or another branch of the government is given responsibility for establishing and managing the money system. In the United States, the Constitution gives that power to the Congress.

Does the Constitution, which mentions only the power to "coin" money, give Congress sole power over all money?

Answer: Yes, Article 1, section 8, paragraph 5, of the Constitution provides that "the Congress shall have power to coin money, regulate the value thereof, and of foreign coin." It is generally agreed that only the word "coin" was used because there were no banks of issue in the country at the time the Constitution was written, and the Founding Fathers assumed that coins would always meet the needs of lawful money.

Over the past century and a half, many questions about Congress powers over the Nation's money system have arisen, and the Supreme Court has upheld the proposition that "whatever power there is over the currency is vested in the Congress."

When was the U. S. dollar convertible into gold?

Answer: For almost 100 years prior to 1934, except for 18 years during and following the Civil War.

Did the gold dollar mean that all of the currency and bank deposits could be converted to gold?

Answer: Yes, but in theory only. Anybody who actually asked to have his dollars converted to gold would get his gold. But if everybody had demanded gold for his dollars, the story would have been quite different. There was never enough gold in the country at any time to supply gold in exchange for all the dollars.

Has the United States actually gone off the gold standard?

Answer: Yes, except in its international transactions. The "gold standard" usually means that people may exchange their paper money for gold whenever they desire. Today, the dollar can be exchanged for gold only in international transactions, although we still define the dollar in terms of gold. In other words, when we owe foreigners money, they may collect it either in gold or in goods or services.

Why is it important for the country to have the right amount of money?

Answer:

When the Federal Reserve does not allow enough money to be created, there will be, in effect, empty seats in the economy (just as in a theater). Plants do not operate at full capacity, some people cannot find jobs, and real wealth, which might have been created, is not created. Under these conditions, industry reduces its investment in new and more efficient productive facilities; and the search of scientists, experimenters, and technicians for new and better ways of doing things slows down.

If the official money managers do not permit the amount of money to increase as rapidly as the monetary needs of a growing economy, then growth will be stunted by monetary deficiency, high interest rates, and continuous unemployment looms. On the other hand, an economy can suffer equally from too much money relative to its needs. An overabundance of money by spurring demand presses the economy to produce beyond its capacity.

When this occurs, the extra demand cannot bring about an increase in production, but only an increase in prices. Inflation erupts.

How is the "money supply" defined?

Answer: The "money supply" is most usually defined as the demand deposits in commercial banks of the country, plus the currency and coin in circulation outside these banks. This is the definition which Federal Reserve officials and most professional economists use when they have in mind a question of how much money is "right" for any level of economic activity.

Demand deposits (checking accounts) in commercial banks, plus currency and coins, make up, in theory at least, the total amount of money which could be spent at any one time. Many of us have, of course, money deposited with savings and loan associations, in the hands of life insurance companies, in pension funds, and so forth. Why isn't this money included in the "money supply"?

It could be, or a least some of it could, and there are times when economists find it convenient to use a broader definition of money than the usual one. But a moment's thought will show that these types of money, savings and loan deposit, for example, are not immediately available to make a purchase. A savings and loan account is not a checking account and the depositor first has to withdraw the money from the bank before it can be used.

In addition, all the money deposited with a savings and loan association eventually is redeposited in a commercial bank or remains in the form of currency and coin outside the commercial banks. So this money is already counted in the "money supply". The same is true for money going to an insurance company, pension fund or other non-commercial-bank financial institution.

Individuals' accounts with these institutions are not included in the "money supply," then, to avoid counting the same money twice.

How is money created?

<u>Answer</u>: There are two important types of deposits to keep in mind. Ordinary checking deposits kept by the public in commercial banks. And commercial bank deposits, <u>reserves</u>, on the books of the Federal Reserve.

Where do the commercial banks get these reserves? By and large, the vast bulk of the reserves are created by the Federal Reserve and credited to the account of the various commercial banks. Created by the Federal Reserve? Yes, and this should not be too much of a mystery. For the Federal Reserve is the banker's bank. When a bank borrows from the Federal Reserve, the Reserve increases the amount of the bank's reserve account with it by the amount of the loan, and new bank reserves are thereby created.

Now the first step into the money fabricating mechanism can be taken. How can an increase in the money supply come about? One-way, there are others as will be seen, is to have the Federal Reserve make a loan to a commercial bank. When the Reserve does this, the commercial bank's deposit with the Federal Reserve increase, and the commercial bank is now richer.

It has more money, equal to the value of the loan on deposit with the Federal Reserve. Technically, the bank's "reserve account" increases. Its reserve account deposits are "high powered" dollars for they have the power to generate a multiple expansion of money: i.e., currency plus demand deposits.

With an increase in its reserves, the bank can now increase its own lending. And the reason it can is that ours is a "<u>fractional reserve</u>" system, with reserves substituting for the goldsmith's gold. When a bank's reserves increase, it can increase its lending by some amount. And these loans take the form of increased demand deposits at the commercial bank, and increases in "checkbook money." So, by an increase in reserves, the money supply can be increased.

Turn from the money supply, for the moment, back to the reserve-creating mechanism. The example of reserve creation ran in terms of a loan from the Federal Reserve to the commercial bank. Actually, the Federal Reserve has alternative ways of increasing reserves. A most important one is by the purchase of securities, specifically U. S. Government securities.

This is what happens: When the Federal Reserve buys, say, $1 million of Government securities, from a nonbank bond dealer, it gives the bond dealer a check in the amount of $1 million, drawn on the Federal Reserve. The bond dealer will deposit this check with his bank. The bank will credit the dealer's checking account with $1 million. Reserves have increased by $1 million through the securities purchase by the Federal Reserve.

Where does the Federal Reserve get the money with which to create bank reserves? Answer: It doesn't "get" the money, it creates it. When the Federal Reserve writes a check for a Government bond it does exactly what any bank does, it creates money. The only difference is that the Federal Reserve's check ends up as an increase in reserves for the banking system, an increase in bank deposits with the Federal Reserve, as well as an increase in some private bondholder's checking account at his commercial bank.

A Federal Reserve purchase creates two increases in deposits at once, a bank's deposit with the Federal Reserve, and a deposit with a private commercial bank.

Unlike the commercial bank, the Federal Reserve does not have any money of its own deposited somewhere else on the basis of which it makes its loans or security purchases. It creates money purely and simply by writing a check. And if the recipient of the check wants cash, then the Federal Reserve can oblige him by printing the cash, Federal Reserve notes, which the check receiver's commercial bank can then hand over to him.

The Federal Reserve, in short, is a total moneymaking machine. It can print money, if that is what is demanded, or issue checks. It never has a problem of making its checks "good" because, of course, it can itself print the $5 and $10 bills necessary to cover the check.

Obviously, this power to create and print money could only be given to the Federal Reserve by Congress. This is the case: The Federal Reserve System is an agency of Congress authorized to create money.

All of the examples were illustrations of the manufacture of money. But the banking system can also destroy money. The process is the exact reverse of money creation. When a bank repays a loan to the Federal Reserve, it writes a check to the System which "collects" the check by deducting the amount of money from the bank's deposit with the Federal Reserve.

The banks's reserves are then decreased and the bank must begin contracting deposits---calling in loans or selling investments---to get back within the permitted deposit limit for its shrunken reserves. And the calling of loans or selling of investments will start a deposit contraction process, the reverse image of the expansion process described earlier.

Perhaps it is now clear why the banking system was called a two-layer system earlier in the chapter. Expansion or contraction of the money supply occurs first, through a change in reserves which the commercial banks hold, and, second by the commercial banks responding to their changed reserve situation by changing the amount of "checkbook money" outstanding.

With a two-part system, the Federal Reserve can change the money supply by operating on any one of the two layers.

What are "open market operations"?

Answer: "Open market operations" refer to the Federal Reserve System's buying and selling of Government securities in what is called the open market. In these buying and selling operations, the Federal Reserve Bank of New York acts as agent for the entire System. The other regional Reserve banks are later informed of changes in the System's port folio and, as a corollary, of their respective port folios.

The purpose of buying or selling Government securities is to expand or contract bank reserves and, hence, to expand or contract the amount of money and credit available to business and consumers.

What is the "open market"?

Answer: The so-called open market consists of 21 private dealers in U.S. Government securities with whom the Federal Bank of New York trades. Several of these dealers are big New York and Chicago banks.

The other dealers are firms centered in the Wall Street area which specialize in buying and selling securities.

The bond dealers, incidentally, may have purchased the bonds from an insurance company, from an individual, an industrial corporation, a commercial bank, or any other financial institution, or from the US Treasury.

How much money can the private banks create when the Federal Reserve creates $1 billion of bank reserves or high-powered money?

Answer: At the present time the Federal Reserve's rules permit member banks of the Federal Reserve System to create $7 for each $1 of reserves credited to their accounts with the Federal Reserve banks. That means that under the present rules relating to fractional reserve banking, when the Federal Reserve System gives its member banks an added $1 billion of these reserves, these banks can create up to $7 billion of new money credited to the accounts of their customers. The banks create this new money by the process already explained.

For whom does the Federal Reserve purchase or sell gold?

Answer: Only the U. S. Treasury purchases and sells gold. The Federal Reserve handles these transaction, acting as agent for the Treasury.

What are the sources of the gold purchased by the Treasury?

Answer: To a small extent the Treasury purchases newly mined gold. Most gold is purchased from foreign "central banks" and, similarly, most of the Treasury's sales of gold are to foreign central banks.

91

Why does the Treasury purchase gold?

Answer: The small amounts of newly mined gold are purchased by the Treasury to add to the Nation's monetary gold stock. Since foreign central banks holding any of our currency may call upon the Treasury to convert the currency to gold, it is important to have enough gold to meet any such claims that may be presented.

But, most of the Treasury's purchases, and sales, of gold are made from and to foreign central banks. These purchases and sales reflect the fortunes of our international balances of payments with foreign countries.

How does the Federal Reserve create bank reserves when it purchases gold for the Treasury?

Answer: It is a duplication of what happens when the Federal Reserve purchases Government bonds in the open market. When the Treasury buys either newly mined gold or gold from a foreign central bank, bank reserves are expanded to exact amount of the purchase.

Since foreign banks can redeem dollars for gold, why don't foreigners turn in all of their dollars in exchange for gold?

Answer: Because money in the form of gold draws no interest; it simply has storage expenses. Foreign central banks would prefer to have dollar credits in this country because these can be invested in interest-bearing securities or dividend-earning stocks.

Who determines how much currency and coin is issued?

<u>Answer</u>: This depends on the behavior of individuals and business firms. The amount of currency and coins in circulation depends upon how convenient individuals and business firms find coins and currency, rather than bank deposits, in carrying on trade. Money is created first in the form of bank deposits, and most money remains in this form.

When someone goes to the bank and asks for currency, "cash," in exchange for a check, the bank gives him the currency and reduces his checking account by the amount of the check. Then as the bank needs "cash" itself to meet its depositor's demands, it gets the cash from the Federal Reserve by having its deposit reduced.

What would happen if the customers of a bank all demanded to have their deposits in cash?

<u>Answer</u>: The bank would be in much the same difficulty that the goldsmith bankers got into when their customers came in and demanded the gold. As we have seen, in the average bank today, customers' claims for cash, that is their deposit balances, amount to about seven times the bank's reserves. Even if the bank drew out all of its reserves in cash, it would have only one-seventh enough money to pay its depositors.

The difference between a member bank of the Federal Reserve System and the goldsmith bankers, however, is that the Federal Reserve will come to the rescue of a bank which gets into such a difficulty and lend it enough reserves to pay off its customers.

If the Government can issue bonds, why can't it issue money and save the interest?

<u>Answer</u>: A few clear-headed and firm individuals, such as Abraham Lincoln, have insisted that the

93

Government can. The late Thomas Edison once stated the matter this way:

> If our nation can issue a dollar bond it can issue a dollar bill. The element that makes the bond good makes the bill good also. The difference between the bond and the bill is that the bond lets money brokers collect twice the amount of the bond and an additional 20 per cent, whereas the currency pays nobody but those who contribute directly in some useful way.
>
> It is absurd to say that our country can issue $30 million in bonds and not $30 million in currency. Both are promises to pay. But one promise fattens the usurers, and the other helps the people.

* * * * * * * *

It is with this poignant assessment of money creation by Thomas Edison that I want to conclude my quoting from "A Primer on Money." Edison's observation poses the real contradiction that exists between the nation's monetary needs financed by the private banker's interest-bearing debt or its needs financed by the sovereign people without incurring either interest and debt.

Later we will be quoting at length Edison's challenge to public funding when The New York Times interviewed him.

I have been quite generous in quoting from **A Primer on Money.** In my estimation this small book is priceless in expounding the functioning of our privately owned and controlled Federal Reserve System. It is a book that should be in every high school, college and public library.

94

No force in our society impinges so devastatingly on the lives and future of the people than our central banking system!

It should now be clear in our minds how the Federal Reserve System inherently can increase or decrease the amount of money in the society. Let us give some thought to what happens. . . .

16

"Boom and bust"

THE AVERAGE American has little understanding of the causes of either inflation or deflation of his nation's money and credit. The fundamental causes of the change in value of the dollar entirely escape him because he has been purposely kept ignorant of how private banking functions.

The purpose now is to cast some light on the twin mysteries of inflation and deflation and how the real culprit of destroyed purchasing power is the privately owned and controlled banking system. The **Primer** has demonstrated how our money supply can be arbitrarily increased and decreased.

We now need to understand how multi-billions, nigh trillions, of dollars in interest, property and savings are ruthlessly and callously wrested from the consuming public by private debt-merchants.

The fact to be remembered is that the nation's monetary supply is expanded or contracted by loans, which become demand deposits or checking accounts. We learned that private banks do not loan to borrowers other people's savings or the assets of the bank itself. Every credit-dollar that a commercial bank puts into circulation in the form of loans is **new money** that has been created.   It **never existed** before.

We also learned that the "Open Market Committee" of the Federal Reserve has even more direct, arbitrary power to expand or contract the total money supply by the selling or buying of Government securities.   The creation of demand deposits (checkbook money) and the despotic operations of the Open Market Committee, both controlled by the Federal Reserve System, are arbiters of the nation's money and credit.

At any given moment, the purchasing power of the people is the amount of cash, savings and demand deposits in existence. In short, the law of supply and demand applies explicitly to the purchasing value of the unit "dollar." Increase the number of dollars in circulation and there exist high prices and a **cheap dollar.** Decrease the number of dollars in circulation and there exist low prices and a **high dollar.**

It is the manipulation by first creating a cheap dollar, with all its seductive ramifications of easy borrowing and increased indebtedness, and then creating an expensive dollar, with all its detrimental ramifications of foreclosures and destroyed purchasing power, that has resulted in every major depression and panic the nation has known since its inception. The toll paid by the American people throughout their history in hardship and heartache is immeasurable in the wake of such monetary intrigue.

Startling, as it may seem to American workers and consumers, it is impossible, under our present private banking system, to enjoy prosperity, with full employment and production, without a parallel increase in indebtedness. It is impossible to add a single new dollar into the life-blood of our economic system without an individual, or a corporation, or the government going into debt.

And for the privilege of going into debt, each must pay a tribute to the private Shylocks in the form of exorbitant interest!

At this point it should be easy to observe that when the private banking system commences to expand the money supply, making loans easy to get, we have the condition of **inflation,** a lot of new credit dollars in circulation, against which there are no extra provided goods and services.

Immediately, there is a resurgence of business. Production is increased and the unemployed go to work. New businesses are commenced to produce new items, and general prosperity and good times are at hand.

Parenthetically, however, we should note that the expansion of the money supply has not added one iota to the nation's resources, has not added one additional human being to the work force, or added one scintilla to the nation's technological know-how. Momentarily, private banking has performed no other gesture than to release its stranglehold on the nation's ability to produce. The "magnanimity" of its gesture is but prelude to the big steal in the making.

At the point when the nation and its people are saddled with as much indebtedness as "the traffic will bear," the private banks reverse their whole monetary policy. They commence to call in their loans and to restrict all spending. In other words, they arbitrarily bring about a condition of **deflation**. A circumstance has now been deliberately created in which the cash and credit in circulation are less than the goods and services that are available for purchase.

Inventories become stagnant and unmovable. Men and women are thrown out of work. The whole nation has landed in a disastrous depression.

Witness now what has really happened to the people and their government. It is only a small part of the tragic picture to point out the slowdown of the economy, the hunger, the millions unemployed. The real crime of private banking is that while the people and their government incurred their indebtedness during a period of inflation when a dollar was **cheap,** they now have to pay off their debts with a dollar that is **high.**

Human effort throughout the whole spectrum of the economy has been devalued!

This is the harvest time for the private banks and lending institutions. Not only are there unavoidable wholesale foreclosures on homes, farms and small businesses, but every dollar of future earnings, representing increased human effort, is needed to offset public indebtedness.

Hundreds of billions of dollars are added to the coffers of the unscrupulous financiers by thus inflating and deflating the nation's money supply. It is a high price that the people must pay to enjoy only a temporary prosperity. It is the inevitable consequence of a monetary system that is based on debt.

Our lives and our future are beholden to the whims and self-interest of entities that have no concern for the public well-being!

One would be derelict in covering destruction of purchasing power if one did not mention corporate domination of the nation's work capability and the whole area of "price-fixing" in which consumers are robbed of purchasing power. Another area is the destruction of purchasing power by confiscatory taxes, with one-third of the workers' wages going to wastrel bureaucracy.

Most devastating in the loss of purchasing power has been the continuous underwriting of cold and hot wars that were undefined and unnecessary. Of course, even the loss in purchasing power of hundreds of billions of dollars is far overshadowed by the loss of our finest young in bloody conflict.

In both my books **There Is A Way!,** which was published in 1995, and **A Blueprint for Survival**, which was published in 2002, I devote much space and detail to both the above areas. In this book my focus is on the role of private banking in our economy and its devastating effect on our economic lives.

17

Debt and Vampiristic Interest

THE POWER to inflate and deflate the money supply by arbitrarily creating debt-dollars is only half of the picture. Equally devastating to the economy, and thus affecting the lives of all the people, is the whole spectrum of ruinous interest. Every credit-dollar that is put into circulation by the private commercial banks is in the form of interest-bearing indebtedness.

I will try to cover broadly this evil, which has plagued humankind up the centuries, an evil that all major religions, Islam, Christianity and Judaism, in their earliest histories all denounced and forbade. However, we should have a minimal grasp of the pyramiding effect of interest in order to understand the impact it has on our fortunes, our lives, and the stranglehold it currently exerts in suffocating the whole economy.

Willis Harman in his book **Global Mind Change** (Berrett-Koehler Publishers, Inc., San Francisco, 1998) underscores the accumulated interest that results from it being added to every transaction involved in arriving at finished products. He contends that the buyer is unaware that **30 to 50 percent** of all inflated prices are due to the whole chain of interest charges.

These are the total gamut of charges which are assessed from raw stock to refining, to wholesale, to transportation, to seductive advertising and finally to the consumer at the retail store.

The Bureau of Public Debts, U. S. Department of the Treasury, cites interest figures for a twenty-year span of time. During that time the Federal debt increased over 500% from $907,700,000,000 in 1980 to $5,500,000,000,000 **(five and a half trillion dollars)** the beginning of this century. During that period the amount of interest was **5 trillion dollars.**

Since the turn of the New Century the Federal debt has doubled and now reached over **eleven trillion dollars** (February, 2009) with a projected deficit of 500 billion dollars each ensuing year

But that is only the Federal debt. On the Local and State level we deal with similar astronomical burdens as to debt and accumulated interest charges.

When we commence to deal with private debt in terms of consumer debt, mortgage and credit card, we again have debt in trillions of dollars and interest in hundreds of billions. Private debt has been climbing through the decade with household debt nearly doubling to **$6.59 trillion** from $3.55 trillion in 1990.

An article in **Time** magazine, November 3, 2008, entitled "Life Without Credit," cites the total household debt in the United States up 20% since 2005, at the alarming amount of **$13.8 trillion.**

Credit cards are a financial bonanza for the banks especially during depressive times when users have to resort to multiple cards to meet the high interest charges assessed for late payments. Total indebtedness has risen to over **one trillion dollars.**

It is estimated that lending institutions have extracted upwards of **$15 trillion** in interest since the year 1960. But, these charges are just the initial toll. Loss of home, loss of farm, loss of jobs, loss of business and savings are the tolls that are paid when payment on mortgages and loans are delinquent and the nation's debt merchants demand their "pound of flesh".

During the last three months of 2008 3.6 million jobs were lost and in January, 2009 there was a 600,000 loss of jobs for that one month alone. And the prospects are glimmer and bleaker.

Intolerable is the massive loss of jobs. Unemployment is the worst since the Great Depression with over ten million without jobs and over a half million not seeking employment because it is a futile gesture.

Endless Bailout of Wall Street!

THE MASSIVE breakdown of the whole financial house of cards was inevitable! Finally, the nation was ambushed with the bursting of the housing bubble the fall of 2008. Some three million homes had been foreclosed and an additional six million were being threatened.

Fannie Mae and Freddie Mac are the two government sponsored mortgage giants that together hold or guarantee about **5 trillion dollars** in mortgage debt.

700 billion dollars! This was the first underwriting under George W. Bush to bail out Wall Street. An ill-informed and supine Congress passed the bill purported to stop the hemorrhaging of home foreclosures and increasing unemployment.

The irony and tragedy lies in the fact that none of the billions of tax dollars went to help those evicted from their homes or stem the wholesale loss of jobs. They did not go to the people who were suffering and who were promised help! They went to bailout Wall Street!

The major contradiction and deception in the whole picture is that taxpayer's dollars went to the nation's largest banks, insurance companies and investment firms who were the ones whose reckless and irresponsible actions were initially responsible for the melt down of the whole financial network.

The picture of the economic breakdown and the recipients of the hundreds of billions of tax dollars is murky and unclear. The names of top financial culprits, as Goldman Sachs, AIG, Bank of America, Fannie Mae, Freddie Mac, Citigroup, J. P Morgan and others, are prominently known but all the machinations and interrelated connections are missing.

Missing are all the transactions in derivatives and hedge funds in trillions of dollars. Also all the hostile takeovers and deals behind closed doors.

What isn't missing is how vulnerable homebuyers were inveigled to take out subprime mortgages, which the unscrupulous lenders knew would lead to wholesale foreclosures!

The private banks have no desire to own foreclosed homes, farms or small businesses. The vicious cycle is to refinance the foreclosed properties or get new borrowers, insuring a perpetual furtherance of debt and accumulated interest.

This is the abominable aspect of private banking. Always exploiting human effort and toil to fill their non-producing coffers!

And then there is the arrogance and lack of integrity of the CEOs and those in highest positions doling out multiple millions to themselves in bonuses when their institutions are in the throes of bankruptcy.

The next huge bailout is the spending of the other half of the 700 billion dollar original bailout. Secretary of the Treasury, Timothy Geithner, has moved urgently to further bail out the nation's largest banks.

And now with much rhetoric and political bickering by the two political parties, a **789 billion dollar economic stimulus bill** has been passed and there is ongoing partisan debate on what distraught segment of the society should have priority in being helped.

The only bipartisan agreement is that larger and larger bailouts are needed to bring any real relief to the millions losing their homes and the growing spectre of millions without jobs. Some economists and political pundits set the total amount sought to bail out the national economy as exceeding **five trillion dollars.**

As I write, a fiscal budget of **3.6 trillion dollars** for 2009 is being presented to Congress. Most alarming is the projected deficit of **one trillion dollars** the first year but could be that economic loss for each of the **next ten years.**

The foregoing figures of interest and debt overwhelm us as to their debilitating reality. The brain has trouble comprehending the magnitude of debts and interest by simply dealing with statistics covering the plight of a whole nation. It is the stark impact on the individual or single family that is felt with much more sobering reality.

The elderly on Medicare get the full impact of interest inflation when they are forced to limit their purchase of food in order to buy life-sustaining drugs. The same is true when a youngster is sent to college and tens of thousands of dollars are incurred in debt.

And what of the graphic plight of the young buying their first home!

In buying a $100,000 home with a mortgage rate of 8.5 percent for a 30-year period, the couple finds that their total payments are $276,840, an amount that represents an interest accumulation of **$176,840** beyond the value of the home itself

After many years of struggling to have a home of their own, with the added responsibility of raising a family, they are forced to stand helplessly by while a private bank, or other lending institution, wrests the home from them.

And remember that the loan that underwrote the home was not based on anything the bank parted with but was based on the borrower's own working capability or secured by the mortgage that the bank held against the buying couple!

To get a glimpse into the astronomical amounts that the private banks extort out of the economy is to consider a very simple fact. It is that any amount of money loaned at 6% interest doubles itself every 12 years. At 8% interest it doubles itself in 9 years and at 9% it doubles itself in 8 years and so on with increased percentage rates.

It is the foregoing fact, plus the circumstance that the vast bulk of loans by the private banks are simply book entries and are not made up of the deposits of others or assets of the bank itself, that makes interest-taking so insidious, so pernicious and so astronomical.

In an upcoming chapter Professor Soddy will demonstrate how the Frankenstein of interest compounds and expands exponentially.

A new President has been elected.

A HISTORICAL FIRST has occurred with an African American now holding the highest office in the land. The task before him is Herculean in magnitude and challenge. He is young, mentally perceptive, has a deep love for his country, and has the support of the majority of the people who pray that he can be successful in setting the nation aright.

The compelling message that must be foremost in the mind of President Obama is that the nation's economy cannot be fully restored to sanity and fairness until the monetary and credit needs of the society are taken from the private banks and placed exclusively in the hands of the sovereign people's government.

It was Abraham Lincoln who stated:

> *Money is the creature of law, and the creation of the original issue of money should be maintained as an exclusive monopoly of the Nation's Government. . . The privilege of creating and issuing money is not only the supreme prerogative of the Government; it is the Government's greatest opportunity.*

Lincoln took steps to underscore this constitutional concept by the issuance of nearly a half billion dollars of **debt-free** and **interest-free** *Greenbacks*. As we have already covered, the private banks were successful in placing limitations on the newly created issue, and then later when they had secretively bought up the depreciated "Greenback", they pressured Congress to have them redeemed in gold

We have covered chronologically how private central banking systems have been set up throughout the world and how they conspire to control governments and systematically exploit the citizen's work capability. Thus, there is no surprise that the financial breakdown is currently worldwide.

The question that looms so starkly and ominously on the horizon is how can President Obama solve the severe financial meltdown by surrounding himself with the ones who were prominently entrenched officials that led to the collapse?

The Rubins, the Summers, the Geithners, the Emanuels, the Paulsons, the Greenspans, the Bernankes and others constitute Obama's **Brain Trust**. Most got their basic training at Goldman Sachs, one of the nations most powerful investment banks. Some were former Secretaries of the Treasury and while there succeeded in deregulating the whole financial network by overriding the Glass-Segal Act.

Lawrence Summers is now Chief Economic Advisor to Obama. Timothy Geithner is the new Secretary of the Treasury and learned his manipulative skills at the International Monetary Fund and as President of the New York Federal Reserve Bank. Rahm Emanuel fills the critical role of White House Chief of Staff.

The current spending spree of unlimited tax dollars will realize some relief in critical areas, but no telling solution to the financial fiasco that besets the nation.

The ensuing months, and perhaps years, will give us a clearer picture as to whether the nation adopts a new sense of direction and whether it is on track to achieve real financial stability and economic justice!

~ 18 ~

9-inch Ball of gold

AT THIS point we want to focus on interest and its compounding effect exponentially. You will find it incredible and startling. We want to quote from **Wealth, Virtual Wealth and Debt** written by Dr. Frederick Soddy. He was a recipient of the Nobel Prize for chemistry in 1921 and made the important discovery of *isotopes*. We will be quoting at different times from his most important book.

Right now we want to focus on his observation respecting interest. He calls our attention to the ownership of a ball of gold, nine inches in diameter, worth 20,000 pounds in English money (1920s), as an individual's possession.

Soddy observes as follows:

> **As a possession it obeys the laws of conservation of matter and energy. As money in its original sense, something to be exchanged for wealth, it possesses no powers of self-production.**

> **As a hoard or store used to buy goods it would diminish in quantity, like soap when you wash with it. But <u>lent</u> to someone else, and buried out of sight in the vaults of some bank, like seed in the earth or a fowl laying eggs, it reproduces its kind.**

> **If the rate is 5 per cent per annum, it becomes capable of supporting in gentility and perpetual motion a whole family and their heirs and successors after them on 1,000 pounds a year. It <u>may</u> buy a farm and his laborers, out of the increment of which they and our family together**

may be supported for ever after. It rises superior to the laws of physics and now energizes an entirely idle owner.

Soddy taxes our wildest stretch of the imagination and our credulity when he projects the incremental gain of the owner if the owner lends the interest thus changing it from simple to compound interest. This happens:

The revenue of the hypothetical farm is now hypothetically sold for more gold and more farms. In 1070 years out of our 9-inch ball of gold, disposed of in this way, there would arise legal claim to a golden ball equal in size to the earth, and weighing four times as much.

Soddy projects interest taking one step further:

Or if we are to get the best out of both possible worlds, let us maintain our chosen family in the state of somewhat shabby gentility and perpetual motion on 500 pounds a year, "putting by" half the income to "accumulate." After enduring this for four centuries, our family would be in a position to supply a world population of 2,000,000,000 souls each with the same principle as itself started with.

Soddy's projected macrocosm role of interest-bearing debt leaves one slightly perplexed and overwhelmed as to its impact on an economy and consequently on our lives as working and consuming citizens.

The following poem, however, covers the same predatory and unworkable role of interest taking but on a scale that is comprehensible and one that we can relate to. While it has an air of levity, the portrayal of interest as a role in our society is painfully true.

FIVE-PER-CENT

Because I have ten thousand pounds I sit upon my
    stern,
    And leave my living tranquilly for other folks to
    earn.
For in some procreative way that isn't very clear,
Ten thousand pounds will breed, they say, five hundred
    every year.

So as I have a healthy hate of economic strife,
    I mean to stand aloof from it the balance of my life.
And yet with sympathy I see the grimy son of toil,
    And heartily congratulate the tiller of the soil.

I like the miner in the mine, the sailor on the sea,
    Because up to five hundred pounds they sail and
    mine for me.
For me their toil is taxed unto that annual extent,
    According to the holy shibboleth of Five-per-Cent.

So get ten thousand pounds, my friend, in any way you
    can,
And leave your future welfare to the noble Working
    Man.
He'll buy you suits of Harris tweed, an Airedale and a
    car,
Your golf clubs and your morning Times, your whiskey
    and cigar.
He'll cozily install you in a cottage by a stream,
    with every modern comfort, and a garden that's a
    dream.

111

Or if your tastes be urban, he'll provide you with a flat,
  secluded from the clamor of the proletariat.
With pictures, music, easy chairs. a table of good cheer,
  A chap can manage nicely on five hundred pounds a
  year.
And though around you painful signs of industry your
  view,
Why should you work when you can make your money
  work for you?

So I'll get down upon my knees and bless the Working
Man,
  Who offers me a life of ease through all my mortal
  span;
Whose loins are lean to make me fat, who slaves to
  keep me free,
Who dies before his prime to let me round the century;
Whose wife and children toil in turn until their strength
is spent,
  That I may live in idleness upon my five-per-cent.
And if at times they curse me, why should I feel blame?
  For in my place I know that they would do the very
  same.

Aye, though they hoist a flag that's red on Sunday
afternoon,
  Just offer them ten thousand pounds and see them
  change their tune.
So I'll enjoy my dividends and live my life with zest,
And bless the mighty men who first invented
  Interest.

Bar Room Ballads (1940)

Robert William Service

112

Sage of Menlo Park

IT SEEMS MOST TIMELY at this point to print the interview that **The New York Times** had with Thomas Edison. We have covered quite a number of pages with considerable technical language in explaining the abusive power exercised by the Federal Reserve System. It is always a breath of fresh air to reduce such lengthy coverage to simple concepts that are quickly and clearly grasped by the ordinary citizens.

Thomas Edison has done this for us. In his interview with **The New York Times**, Edison has given us an indisputable picture of the contrast of the funding of the debt-money by private banking and debt-free funding by the sovereign people as provided for by the Constitution.

The interview is a gem in its simplicity and compelling reasoning!

The interview we are referring to was reported in **The New York Times** for December 6, 1921 and was placed in the Congressional Record of February 11, 1943.

Representative Jerry Voorhis (D. CA) whom we have quoted earlier from his book **"Out of Debt, Out of Danger"** in making the request for the interview to be placed in the Congressional Record stated: "There is one feature of the work of Edison which is not recognized as widely or appreciated as much as his work in the field of science. Edison possessed a clear vision of how absolutely unnecessary it is for the money of the nation to be tied to public or private debt."

Voorhis stated further: "On the occasion of an interview Edison gave at Muscle Shoals when the great dam at that place was being considered for construction, he gave a classic interview on that particular subject, pointing out that the validity of the money of the people depends always on their production of wealth and the taxing power of their nation rather than on any other thing."

The following excerpts from the interview that was placed in the Congressional Record allude to a plan by Henry Ford that clearly points out the basic difference between funding by the currency (non-debt) method instead of by (debt-creating) bond issues:

> **Mr. Edison reiterated his belief expressed yesterday, that it was a good plan and that if once "the currency method is tried in raising money for public improvements, the country will never go back to the bond method. . . . Now here is Ford proposing to finance Muscle Shoals by an issue of currency. Very well, let us suppose for a moment that Congress follows his proposal. Personally, I don't think Congress has imagination enough to do it, but let us suppose it does.**

> **"The required sum is authorized, say $30,000,000. The bills are issued directly by the Government, as all money ought to be. When the workmen are paid off they receive these United States bills. Except that perhaps the bills may have the engraving of a water dam, instead of a railroad and a ship, as some of the Federal Reserve notes have.**

"They will be the same as any other currency put out by the Government, that is, they will be money. They will be based on the public wealth already in Muscle Shoals, and their circulation will increase that public wealth, not only the public money but the public wealth, real wealth.

"When these bills have answered the purpose of building and completing Muscle Shoals, they will be retired by the earnings of the power dam. That is, the people of the United States will have all that they put into Muscle Shoals and all that they can take out for centuries, the endless wealth-making water power of that great Tennessee River, with no tax and no increase of the national debt."

Mr. Edison was then asked what if Congress does not go along with the foregoing debt-free proposal. To which he replied:

"Well, Congress must fall back on the old way of doing business. It must authorize an issue of bonds. That is, it must go out to the money brokers and borrow enough of our own national currency to complete great national resources, and we then must pay interest to the money brokers for the use of our own money. That is to say, under the old way any time we wish to add to the national wealth, we are compelled to add to the national debt.

"Now, that is what Henry Ford wants to prevent. He thinks it is stupid, and so do I, that for the loan of $30,000,000 of their own money the people of the United States should be compelled to pay $60,000,000, that is what it amounts to, with interest. People who will not turn a shovelful of dirt nor contribute a pound of material will collect more money from the

United States than will the people who supply the material and do the work.

The most salient and clarifying insight as to debt-free funding came at this juncture of the interview when Edison emphasized the following point:

"But here is the point: If our nation can issue a dollar bond, it can issue a dollar bill. The element that makes the bond good makes the bill good, also. The difference between the bond and the bill is that the bond lets the money brokers collect twice the amount of the bond and an additional 20 percent, whereas the currency pays nobody but those who directly contribute to Muscle Shoals in some useful way.

"If the Government issues bonds, it simply induces the money brokers to draw $30,000,000 out of the other channels of trade and turn it into Muscle Shoals; if the Government issues currency, it provides itself with enough money to increase the national wealth at Muscle Shoals without disturbing the business of the rest of the country. And in doing this, it increases its income without adding a penny to its debt.

"It is absurd to say that our country can issue $30,000,000 in bonds and not $30,000,000 in currency. Both are promises to pay; but one promise fattens the usurer, and the other helps the people. If the currency issued by the Government were no good, then the bonds issued would be no good either.

"It is a terrible situation when the Government to increase the national wealth, must go into debt and submit to ruinous interest charges at the hands of men who control the fictitious value of gold.

"Look at it another way. When the Government issues bonds, the brokers will sell them. The bonds will be negotiable; they will be considered as gilt-edged paper. Why? Because the Government is behind them, but who is behind the Government? The people. Therefore, it is the people who constitute the basis of Government credit.

"Why then cannot the people have the benefit of their own gilt-edged credit by receiving noninterest-bearing currency on Muscle Shoals, instead of the bankers receiving the benefit of the people's credit in interest-bearing bonds?

"The people must pay anyway; why should they be compelled to pay twice, as the bond system compels them to pay? The people of the United States always accept their Government's currency.

"If the United States Government will adopt this policy of increasing its wealth without contributing to the interest collector—for the whole national debt is made up of interest charges—then you will see an era of progress and prosperity in this country such as could never have come otherwise."

Mr. Edison was asked, "Are you going to have anything to do with outlining this proposed policy?"

"I am just expressing my opinion as a citizen. Ford's idea is flawless. They won't like it. They will fight it, but the people of this country ought to take it up and think about it. I believe it points the way to many reforms and achievements which cannot come under the old system."

117

We have quoted at some length Edison's interview in **The New York Times** because the thinking of Edison and Ford encapsulates in a handful of paragraphs the most basic flaw in private banking. The sovereign people are unable to release their full work capability to do projects in the public interest **without incurring unpayable interest-bearing debt.**

There is no thinking more crucial and imperative in dealing with the needs of the society than what is embodied in the Edison interview. The cardinal premise brought out in the interview is that a nation should only be limited in what it can do by its resources, its human element, its machines and technology. Debt-free funding should come into existence automatically for all enterprises.

What a breath of fresh air, and joyous sense of relief, if currently the millions suffering the tragedy of Katrina, the millions enduring the onslaught of flooding along the Mississippi, the millions being cast out of their homes and the millions without jobs awoke one morning and the nation's leaders had invoked the debt-free funding that Edison presented and a new economic dawn had blessed the nation!

This isn't mental fantasy, or the figment of an irrational mind! All that is required is a nation awakening to the realization that it is laboring under a false financial and economic structure, all created by the minds and hands of those seeking usurped power and unearned profits by denying the majority the fruits of their labor.

All we have to do is substitute all the public needs of the society for Muscle Shoals. All are enterprises. The only difference is the magnitude of operations. It

118

merits our indulgence to repeat the salient point that Edison made which is the capstone to the whole unique interview. It is this:

> If our nation can issue a dollar bond, it can issue a dollar bill. The element that makes the bond good makes the bill good, also. The difference between the bond and the bill is that the bond lets the money brokers collect twice the amount of the bond and an additional 20 percent, whereas the currency pays nobody but those who directly contribute to Muscle Shoals in some useful way.

It is this fundamental thinking on public funding that gives us real insight as to how our nation has progressively, since its inception, gone deeper and deeper into debt despite its constant perfecting of both its science and technology. Three quarters of a century ago, Congressman Charles Lindbergh in his book **Your Country at War,** which we quoted earlier, underscored the same contradiction in terms of the "Money Trust" controlling the nation's money and credit and preventing the funding of its work capability.

In the chapter "Debt and Vampiristic Interest" I briefly gave thought to the pervasive interest-indebtedness that has economically strangled the nation. However, citing the nation's total indebtedness does not give us the tragic picture in human terms along with the destruction of constitutional and inherent rights.

~ 20 ~
The human tragedy

IN THIS CHAPTER we want to give some realistic thought to the suffering and economic injustice caused by the privately owned and controlled Federal Reserve System. In conjunction with predatory and exploitive private capitalism tens of millions are denied the most basic needs to survive.

We need to understand emotionally the human tragedy within the hearts and minds of those suffering.

We need to empathize with the victims and let them know that **There is a Way** (my book published in 1995) to economic liberation and an abundant existence.

We need to rally the cohorts for a righteous onslaught on the citadels of the wrong doers. An onslaught that embodies definitive proposals that eradicates all aspects of usurped power!

We need to reach into the minds and hearts of those who endure suffering and mistreatment and walk in their footsteps so we are not just dealing with alarming statistics but with blood and flesh human beings desperately trying to survive another day.

According to the Report on **Hunger in America** by Tufts University 12 million children go to bed each night suffering the pangs of hunger. Their gnawing stomachs cry out for nourishment. Mothers stand helplessly by amidst stores and warehouses bulging with foodstuffs.

This is human tragedy on the most innocent strata of our society. However, it is but the heart of the problem. Upwards of forty million people in this nation live in poverty and it is a scourge that has afflicted the nation interminably for the larger part of the nation's existence.

Some thirty million endure mental breakdown from the stresses of the society. Over 2 million are chronically mentally ill and abandoned. One quarter of a million end in jail without having treatment of any kind. And finally, the tragedy of the youngest in our society, and the elderly, ending their lives by suicide.

For a number of years I was the president of the Hamilton County, Indiana, Mental Health Association but much of my effort was on the state level. We primarily dealt with the chronically mentally ill. These were those on the bottom of the totem pole and were the ones who had been in and out of the state institutions. Most were prone to alcohol and drugs.

We set up group homes giving loved ones respite in taking care of those with troubled minds. The state of the art in the established Mental Health Centers was to medicate the sick and keep them subdued without any real approach to their potential for becoming self-sufficient citizens.

In the past two decades the suicide rate among children ages 10 to 14 has doubled. Eight percent of students in grades 9 through 12 attempted suicide during 1999. Twenty million children nation-wide attend schools that are falling apart and in need of repair and updating.

Prior to the bursting of the housing bubble, there already were two million homeless sleeping in alleys and cardboard boxes were their only shelter. Half were women and children and one-third were veterans who had put their lives at stake in behalf of their country.

As I write, the beginning of 2009, three million families have been added to the roster of the homeless having been evicted from their homes by foreclosures. Evictions threaten millions more and the most basic need, a home, in raising children has been shattered.

And health care? It is incredible and unacceptable, that the richest nation in the world (at least potentially) cannot provide for its sick and injured. Forty-four million Americans are without medical insurance. And this lack, striking at the very core of existence, is further aggravated by loss of jobs and foreclosures of businesses.

And what about the right to work? The need to work? Without income, all needs and wants are magnified! Recent statistics cite unemployment at a rate of over 9% with the most stricken areas of 15% to 20%. The tragic situation cites an overall jobless calamity of 11,000,000 who futilely seek work. And this huge unemployment does not count the two million who in frustration quit looking for employment or those holding just part-time jobs.

The future is ominous and bleak. Since September, 2008, 3.6 million have become unemployed, and just during the month of January, 2009, 600,000 jobs have been terminated.

The thrust of the whole economy is "maximization of profit" for the 5% of shareholders at the top and monopolistic power for fewer and fewer corporate giants. There is brutal indifference to whether or not a family has a provider to keep loved ones together.

Highest paid jobs are lost and irreplaceable by corporate "downsizing" in all the areas of production, service and management. "Outsourcing", transferring technical jobs to countries like China and India, add to the growing list of the unemployed.

The major contradiction that exists in the nation is the presence of millions unemployed at the same time that the nation has critical work to be done. How can there be justification in having millions futilely searching for work when the nation's water supplies, sewage systems, bridges and highways are crumbling?

Or the dire need for building low-income housing and erecting adequate and updated medical and educational institutions?

Or the need to clean up the countless areas of pervading toxic pollution? The nation's lakes and rivers are unsafe to drink and unsafe to swim in because of contamination.

Disposal of tons of low and high radioactive material still remains unresolved. Estimates run into hundreds of billions of dollars to clean up contaminated material at nuclear power plants.

And disposal of the deadly VX nerve agent, the country's most hazardous chemical weapon, has not as yet been resolved. At Newport, Indiana four million pounds are stored. One drop on the skin could kill a person in eight to ten minutes. And there are three other sites in the nation.

A whole nation, publicly and privately, floundering in a sea of trillions of dollars in unpayable indebtedness which is being passed on to the unborn. Federal debt is now over **9 trillion dollars** (summer, 2008) with 400 billion dollars annually to service the debt.

Similar astronomical indebtedness burdens State and Local governments, which are forced to cut needed programs in Medicaid, Head Start and school and hospital construction

Consumer debt has reached the staggering burden of approaching **7 trillion dollars,** doubling since 1990. Credit card debt has soared over **1 trillion dollars.**

The ultimate injustice is the lender wresting the home, the farm, the business from their owners when it is the bank that caused the stringent economic conditions leading to the foreclosures.

Increasingly, the family farm, the local retailer and the small manufacturer are being driven out of the economy while there are larger and larger corporate mergers, unrestrained by the nation's anti-trust laws. (Sherman Act and Clayton Act) .

It is a time of unbridled greed and arrogance of power reflected by the behavior of corporate CEOs in conglomerates like Global Crossing, Enron, WorldCom, Tyro, Adelphia and other corporate giants. While charges of "cooking" books, setting up bogey entities, and the siphoning off tens of billions for themselves, since the collapse of Enron, many have been charged but only one or two have gone to jail.

The other side of the coin, however, has meant tens of thousands of workers downsized or laid off, their stock investments undercut and their pensions destroyed.

During the George W. Bush Administration, 3 million industrial workers have become unemployed and face the bleak prospect of finding jobs.

The mania of corporate mergers has increased the power of monopolistic giants to control a captive Congress both electively and legislatively. Along with self-serving privileged legislation they have succeeded in precluding remedial legislation that would achieve economic justice for the majority of the citizens.

An informed citizenry respecting the literal steps for change is imperative. Concentrated control of the nation's media (radio, TV, Internet, newspapers, magazine, etc.) is now owned and controlled by **six conglomerates.** They determine what the citizens shall see, hear or read and thus have made a hollow mockery of democracy.

We have become a total society permeated with sleaze, scams, frauds, swindles and ethical and moral breakdown.

We have become a total society engulfed in violence, assaults, and homicides and one is unable to find safety on the highways, on the streets, in the schools, in the workplaces or even in one's home.

The most serious abusive power exercised by corporate lobbyists controlling government is the sending of the nation's finest young women and men to give their lives in undefined wars that have nothing to do with the nation's safety!

The most heart rendering is the prospect of inviting new life into a society, and world, so polluted, violent and defiled.

The foregoing is largely statistical in the areas of economic injustice and human suffering. We need to feel empathy with the victims and endure their pain and economic hardships. Most importantly we hope that righteous indignation will come to the fore as more and more people give thought to what has befallen this nation.

We hope that you have been able to keep in mind the interview with Edison. It should give you an insight as to the role that private banking has played in corporate take-over and the resultant injustices and hardships.

Interest-bearing funding exceeds all other evils in our society in terms of the suffering and oppression it has caused. When sufficient numbers of people clearly understand the exploitive and brutal role it has played, it may be difficult to hold an outraged people in check as they clamor for both restitution and an end to every vestige of debt-money.

This ultimate state of mind will usher in a society that underscores both economic justice and peace!

In the next chapter we want to enlarge the thinking of Dr. Frederick Soddy whom we have already quoted. It is important that we acquaint ourselves more intensively with his incisive thinking in his book **Wealth, Virtual Wealth and Debt.**

~ 21 ~
"Wealth, Virtual Wealth and Debt"

IN DR. SODDY'S BOOK we get precise demarcations as to the meaning of what is real wealth, virtual wealth and interest-bearing debt. The reader comes to grasp the role each plays in our economy. Most graphically, he or she comes to understand how private banking exploits and controls the economic well-being and actual destiny of the people.

A brief introduction to Dr. Soddy's achievements in research and science should be noted because it reflects the precision and logic which he later applied to his economic thinking. This writer has found that persons involved in fields that embody disciplined thought in research and embodies varying aspects of "systems engineering" have come forth with the most rational observations and conclusions.

Frederick Soddy was born at Eastbourne, Sussex, England on September 2, 1877. He passed on in 1956 after a lifetime of research into the chemistry of radioactive substances and his investigations into the origin and nature of isotopes.

Soddy made his major scientific contribution in 1913 with his formulation of the concept of isotopes, which stated that certain elements exist in two or more forms which have different atomic weights but which are chemically indistinguishable.

His important books include Radioactivity (1904), *The Interpretation of Radium* (1909), *The Chemistry of the*

Radioactive Elements (1912-1914), *Matter and Energy* (1912), *Science and Life* (1920), *The Interpretation of the Atom* (1949) and *Atomic Transmutation* (1953).

The Nobel Prize in Chemistry was presented to Dr. Soddy in 1921 with these words:

"Professor Soddy, The Royal Swedish Academy of Sciences, of which institution you have for several years been a highly valued member, is sure that it is acting in complete accordance with the opinion of the scientific world in awarding to you Nobel Prize in Chemistry for 1921, on account of your important contributions to our knowledge of the radioactive bodies of your pioneer works on the existence and nature of isotopes."

"It is with sincere gratification that I have the honor, on behalf of the Academy, to beg you to receive this prize from the hands of His Majesty, who has been graciously pleased to undertake to present to you."

What Is Real Wealth?

SODDY emphasizes and underscores throughout his book that real wealth inexorably must relate to products and services. The scientific equation of creating true wealth is simply human skill and technological know-how combining with earth's bounty and limitless energy.

All forms of credit, the whole spectrum of interest-bearing debt, are varying levels of **virtual wealth** and are the components of monetary systems that have been foisted throughout the centuries on the people unaware of their economic enslavement.

Under the heading "Wealth as a Form of Energy, Its Unlimited Productibility" we get a clear understanding of what wealth is in its most basic makeup. We quote:

If we have available energy, we may maintain life and produce every material requisite necessary. That is why the flow of energy should be the primary concern of economics. In a world which has adequate supplies of energy, scientific knowledge and inventions for utilizing it, and the man-power able and willing to perform the necessary duties and services, poverty and destitution are purely artificial institutions, due to ignorance of the principles of government, actively, if not deliberately, fostered for class ends by legal conventions confounding wealth with debt.

But to people who think of wealth not in terms of energy and human endeavor, but in terms of money-tokens, there seems to be nothing incongruous in the continuance of the acute economic suffering in which Europe has been plunged, nor any evidence of failure in the most elementary function of government in the spectacle of unemployment and poverty at one and the same time."

Under the subtitle "The Dangers of Money" Soddy stresses, as we have stressed throughout this book, that wealth has to have intrinsic worth. It has to be directly related to human effort. When money relates to debt or bank created purchasing power it removes itself from true wealth. We quote:

Money, or some equivalent, is, in consequence, a necessity in any civilization or community above the stage where everyone produces all that he or she consumes. But it is a dangerous necessity,

129

for all that, only too apt to engender in the body politic social diseases potent enough to bring the proudest nations to the dust.

It substitutes for the natural inalienable right of the worker to the produce of his toil a vague generalized claim upon the totality of the fruits of the community's efforts, a highly indefinite quantity, which opens the door to every kind of abuse.

The instability of money and its fluctuation in purchasing power always results when it is not based on, or not related directly to, human toil. We quote:

The variation of the purchasing power of money exposes the community to wholesale injustice on the one side and undeserved gain on the other, as assuredly as if the one set had been despoiled of their belongings by the other by robbery and violence.

But worse than all, it paves the way to the economic subjugation of humanity to monetary power because of the confusion in the minds of people between money and wealth. By substituting for the "conception of a realized amount" "a periodical receipt" of an infinitude of future interest payments, it tries to condemn to eternal slavery generations not yet born.

It is therefore of the utmost importance that all those who wish to understand social problems should understand and make themselves masters of the subject of money.

In this same vein of thinking, Dr. Soddy makes a most telling comparison:

It certainly does seem odd to a tyro to discover that the law proceeds with the utmost severity against the fraudulent counterfeiter for uttering new money tokens, but allows the banks in effect to create it wholesale to lend at interest by these methods, which is a far more profitable business and infinitely more serious in its consequences to the general community than the counterfeiting.

To any other age it would have been the most obvious form of treason against the State.

Under the sub-title "Democracy and the Issue of Money" Soddy quotes President Wilson who belatedly learned too late in 1916: "'A great industrial nation is controlled by its system of credit . . . our system of credit is concentrated. The growth of the nation and all our activities are in the hands of a few men . . . *who can chill and check and destroy our economic freedom.*"

Soddy follows up by stating: "If he had called a spade a spade, and instead of talking of a 'system of credit' had revealed what the term conceals, and said the *'creation and destruction of our money,'* even a bright child with no more than a school knowledge of history could have understood him."

In a crisp and challenging reaction Soddy states the following:

So ends Democracy in an absolute strangle-hold by a few unknown men! At least we have the right to know who our rulers really are, even if it means their unearthing again as much of their reburied gold as will make them crowns.

To seek them out is to find no one in the least resembling the sort of person a great scientific empire or republic would have voluntarily chosen to throttle them, but a number of pettifogging relics and penny bankers mopping and mowing about gold! Away with them! Let the great nation get on with their job."

There is real satisfaction in reading Dr. Soddy's 350 page book "Wealth, Virtual Wealth and Debt" because as a world-renowned scientist his analysis of money and private banking are so logical, compelling and authentic. Also, there is much satisfaction in getting the perspective of an English author in that it meshes basically with what we have presented from the American viewpoint.

In addition, Soddy has given us an added dimension, a most salient incite, in understanding private banking by distinguishing between what is real wealth and what are the deceptive substitutes.

In our coverage of the Federal Reserve System we cited how it was foisted on us by International Banking Interests. Clearly, there was a deliberate and calculated effort to install in America a **Central Banking System** as the Rothchilds had already succeeded in doing on the other side of the Atlantic.

Dr. Soddy poses the question of "conspiracy" in the following manner:

> **The Westerner is not exactly the quickest in the uptake where the elusive principle of Virtual Wealth is concerned. It has escaped the purview of the professed theoretical economists, who seem to have remained entirely oblivious of the profound changes going on under their eyes in the very nature of money.**
>
> **Conspiracy or not, there can be little question that the power these discoveries have put into the hands of financiers will, if not controlled,**

enable them to their own time and choice effectively to conquer the world.

But conscious conspiracy or not, and whether one race rather than another is responsible, there can be no doubt of the fact that finance has already more than half enslaved the world and few, if any, individual, corporations, or even nations can afford to displease the monetary power.

In our next chapter we want to deal with aspects of the international scope of private banking and the governmental and non-governmental entities, which they either directly or indirectly influence or shape

World connections

WE NOW COME to consider the interlocking, interrelated, interdependent, and conspiratorial relationships of private banking throughout the world. Much of these connections and workings are enshrouded in secrecy so that we can only get broad glimpses into their financial machinations. However, it is imperative that we are aware of how our lives and destinies are intermingled with interest-bearing debt on the world stage.

Bilderbergers

THE ORGANIZATION that first comes to mind to those who have evinced some interest in International Banking is the **Bilderbergers.** Most Americans, of course, have not the slightest inkling of who they are and what they do. One might hear the retort, "Is that a new hamburger offering at one of the fast food stands?"

The Bilderbergers are the principal heads of the Central Banks of the world who meet in secret to plan their mutual goals and self-interests. They all have a common goal to sustain the world's corrupt central banking systems and to be ever vigilant of any threats to their exclusive control of national economies.

Leaked information from their secret meetings has revealed some of the calculated goals of the members taking place at their clandestine gatherings. The members are the elitist of the elitist and represent the top echelon not only in international banking but in the dominant corporate monopoly in industry, the media and government on a world scale.

The glimpses we do get into the international schemes of the Bilderbergers are that they are working toward globalization in conjunction with such organizations as the World Trade Organization, the International Monetary Fund and the World Bank.with the spoils going to transnationals with a callous indifference to the economic suffering of the world's majority.

IMF and World Bank

THE STRAIGHT FORWARD TESTIMONY of Ralph Nader on the **International Monetary Fund** before the "General Oversight and Investigations Sub-committee" of the "House of Representatives Committee on Banking and Financial Services" on April 21, 1998 gives us solid insight of the Fund.

He opened his testimony in this manner:

> **The International Monetary Fund is an institution out of control. It is completely unresponsive to the U. S. Congress, which appropriates 18 percent of its monies. In combination with its allies in the Clinton administration, the IMF has misleadingly sought to take advantage of the Asian financial crisis, for which it is to blame, to extract billions of dollars more from the United States, in contrast with its vaunted austerity measures for people in poor countries, the IMF provides free insurance to big bankers, bailing them out when their foreign loans go bad.**

> **The IMF rides roughshod over borrower countries in the Third World, making a mockery**

of attempts to democratically determine macro-economic policy in those nations. And now the IMF is seeking to expand the mission through a stealth amendment to its charter that would require IMF member countries to eliminate restraints on the international flow of capital.

Mr. Nader then proceeds to graphically portray the abysmal failure of U. S. funding to the IMF to achieve "corporate globalization". Bear in mind always that it is the nation's interest-bearing bonds that are given to the Federal Reserve System in order that it can underwrite the funding.

Nader expressed the tragic situation in this manner:

Mr. Chairman, it is increasingly apparent that corporate globalization has scarcely fulfilled its promises. There are innumerable indications of this: the Asian financial crisis, the large and growing U. S. trade deficit; the stagnation in real U. S. wage rates over the last 25 years; the fiat or declining growth rates throughout much of Africa in the past decade and a half; the staggering global concentration of wealth, which, according to a 1996 United Nations Development Program report, has created a condition whereby 358 people collectively control as much wealth as 45 percent of the world's population.

Most disturbing, perhaps, is the shivering of the world's modest attempts of domestic democratic governance in the face of the increasing power of international financial institutions like the IMF, multinational corporations and international currency markets.

Mr. Nader's long and detailed testimony was fraught with mishandling of funds by the IMF and its failure to stabilize the economies of the world, particularly in sustaining the lives of the poorest in the world. He concluded with this broad perspective:

> In the longer term, much more thinking needs to be done to foster a shift away from the corporate globalization model with it emphasis on export-driven economies and foreign-investment dependence. The model throws countries into a perverse competition in which low wages and week environmental standards are rewarded and only multinational corporations are winners; and it leaves nations overly vulnerable to the vagaries of international managers.

> Economies should instead be free to pursue diverse, democratically determined policies, including the mobilization of domestic resources and domestic markets to meet pressing domestic needs.

Another excellent coverage of the IMF and the World Bank is found in the **State of the World 2002** by "The Worldwatch Institute"..A few short paragraphs will suffice since their coverage meshes with the salient points covered by Nader:

> The last few years have also brought growing understanding that World Bank and IMF lending is inextricably linked with the persistent problem of Third World indebtedness, as these institutions are mainly in the business of making loans rather than grants.

> Despite pledges made in Agenda 21 to reduce indebtedness and an energetic campaign for debt cancellation by NGOs, the total debt burden in developing and former Eastern block countries has climbed 34 percent since the Earth Summit, reaching $2.5 trillion in 2000.

Some 17 percent of this total is owed to the World Bank, the IMF, and other public international institutions; 21 percent is owed to national governments, and the remaining 62 percent is owed to commercial banks and other private lenders.

In some heavily indebted countries, such as Zambia, debt service payments now consume as much as 40 percent of total government expenditures. These excessive interest payments are siphoning away resources that could otherwise be spent on much needed social and environmental programs, from HIV prevention and treatment to access to clean water and sanitation.

The financial plot, or intrigue, thickens as we gain knowledge and insight into private banking on the international playing field. In contrast to exploitation on the American scene the manipulative and malicious treatment of the voiceless in undeveloped nations should be doubly condemned.

Clearly, the operation of the International Monetary Fund and World Bank has put profits before workers' rights, human rights and the environment.

The tentacles of interest-bearing debt, with their devastating tolls on human life, reaches out to **every cranny on the earth!**

Trade Treaties

FINALLY, I want to deal with trade agreements and treaties whose policies and actions directly and indirectly bring into play the Federal Reserve System and the debilitating effect of interest-bearing debt.

In major cities like Seattle and Washington hundreds of thousand of concerned individuals and groups have rallied to protest the actions of the International Monetary Fund and World Bank, including Trade Agreements impacting their lives. Such groups, numbering in the hundreds, and representing tens of millions of individuals, have joined together to plead serious causes.

They have rallied behind the just causes of Labor, Environment, Students, Third World, Human Rights, Spiritual and other basic human rights and needs.

While their protests and goals have been focused on the IMF and WB, which we have briefly covered, we now want to focus on our nation's involvement with the Trade Agreements that have impacted the lives of so many millions with equal devastation. They involve corporate globalization, erosion of democracy, loss of millions of jobs, environmental destruction and economic sanctions imposed on the very poorest in the world.

Perhaps the most powerful and most encompassing organization is **WTO** (World Trade Organization) but other organizations, or treaty agreements, like **GATS** (General Agreement on Trade in Services), **FTTA** (Free Trade Area of the Americas) and **NAFTA** (North American Free Trade Agreement) have in collusion or

139

separately caused similar harm to tens of millions in our own land and throughout the world.

Other groups like **EU** (Europe Union), **E8** (made up of the eight main industrial countries in the world) and **OPEC** (monopolist oligarchy of oil companies) have international economic and financial agreements that impact on every citizen in our society.

What we want to highlight is that all such agreements, particularly, those advocating free trade, take their toll in loss of millions of jobs, unavoidable mushrooming indebtedness and a callus insensitivity to the health of the planet.

These agreements encourage and allow corporations to move their operations to foreign lands where they can get "sweat shop" labor and send back to this nation inferior goods. NAFTA alone is responsible for the loss of over **two million jobs.**

These agreements involving exported American workers, and native workers, provide no protection of labor grievance procedures, nor do work conditions abide by laws protecting the work environment and the natural environment..

These agreements are primarily responsible for the trade deficits that have amounted to upwards of **400 billion dollars** for each of the past several years, including. 2004 What does this deficit mean to the nation's workers? Simply this: The American workers are denied the work to produce that amount of goods and products. And consequently denied commensurate wages.

How does the Federal Reserve System come into the picture relative to the impact of the aforementioned trade agreements? The answer is immediate and compelling. Along with the malfunctioning of the private capitalist economic system itself, which causes "downsizing" and loss of millions of jobs, the same culprit is present in trade treaties. In both cases there is the **loss of purchasing power**.

Loss of purchasing power! This is the central core of a flawed economic and financial system. Translated into the day-to-day living of families it touches on their very ability to survive. It touches on the tragic situation of 12 million children going to bed each night suffering from the pangs of hunger when the warehouses are overloaded with food.

It touches on the elderly having to cut down on their life- saving drugs in order to buy food. It touches on 30 million enduring poverty and not knowing how they will make it through the next day. Most seriously, it touches on the jobless who have no paychecks and are dependent on the charity of friends or the handouts of bureaucratic government.

Loss of purchasing power! Here is where the private banking voltures descend on the jobless and the destitute. They are forced to create purchasing power by going into debt. They are asked to mortgage their future earning power to buy goods and services that they had already produced.

It is a field day for the moneylenders. The rougher and more stringent the economy is for the families of this nation, the more favorable and lucrative it is for the debt-merchants of this nation.

This is a human contradiction, and a calculated oppression, that cannot be tolerated. It cries out for public remonstrance and public challenge.

In closing chapters we will learn how the work capability of this nation can be unleashed for an abundant and secure life for every citizen. There will be full implementation of human rights, which will include full employment. No one will be denied the inherent right to always have a job. The advance of technology will simply shorten the workday with ample time for creative endeavors.

Purchasing power will be directly related to full employment and the nation's monetary system will be directly related to the production of all goods and services!

The irrationality of having serious **unmet human needs** when there is unused capacity **to fulfill those needs** is patently unacceptable..

In the next chapter we will briefly recap the chapters covering how this nation ultimately became saddled with the Federal Reserve System. This will give us a jumping off place to commence considering members of Congress, and others, who courageously challenged the iniquities of our central banking system.

Our final chapters will consider proposals that usher in an honest monetary system within an economic framework that unleashes our full productive capacity for an equitable and prosperous life for all the people.

~ 23 ~

Summary

THE PURPOSE of this chapter is to briefly summarize the foregoing pages on the Federal Reserve System. We want to highlight how interest-bearing debt funding has impacted the lives of the citizens since the inception of our nation in 1791. Our coverage will be succinct and basic leaving a re-reading to those who wish a more detailed summary.

Let us start by noting that the nation's money and credit system, leading up to the enactment of the Federal Reserve System and functioning nearly a century after, has not been something delivered to this nation complete and packaged from some entity with divine credentials. We should imbed in our consciousness that the whole complex of money, credit and private banking is a creation of **human entities.**

Secondly, it should be noted that our most outstanding forebears, Jefferson, Adams, Jackson and Lincoln, all grasped, and denounced private banking control of the nation's money and credit. It should be noted that President Lincoln recognized that the exclusive power to provide for our money supply and credit should be vested in the National Government.

He was referring to Article 1, Section 8, Part 5 of the Constitution which states, **"Congress shall have the power to coin money, regulate the value thereof, and of foreign coin."** It was noted that while only the word "coin" was used, because there were no banks of issue at the time, the Supreme Court has upheld the proposition that "whatever power there is over the currency is vested in the Congress."

Lincoln, true to his convictions, followed through and gave the nation its first and only debt-free and interest-free money supply called "Greenbacks".

Lincoln's true assessment of monetary control is worth repeating:

> **Money is the creature of law, and the creation of the original issue of money should be maintained as an exclusive monopoly of the National Government. . . . The privilege of creating and issuing money is not only the supreme prerogative of the Government, it is the Government's greatest opportunity.**

We covered the chronological history of the setting up of the first National Bank in 1791, the struggle over gold and silver backing of the nation's money, and the surreptitious and deceitful enacting of the Federal Reserve Act on December 28, 1913 when many members of Congress were absent.

We covered how the 17th century Goldsmith Bankers discovered "fractional reserve" banking and wrote "gold receipts" for which no gold actually existed. We noted that it was this deceptive practice that would become the core functioning of our Federal Reserve System two centuries later.

We quoted from Frederick Morton's book **The Rothschilds** to get a perspective of how the Rothschilds dominated central banking in European capitals and throughout the world. We quoted:

> **Yet here, in a cramped ghetto dwelling, the great Pauillac wedding had its roots. Here, with a**

yellow star pinned to his caftan, Mayer Amschel Rothschild kept a small store two centuries ago, and married Gutele Schnapper, and raised with her those five incredible sons who <u>conquered the world more thoroughly, more cunningly and more lastingly than all the Caesar's before or all the Hitlers after them.</u>

Such assessment of the Rothschild dynasty gave us a graphic picture of the power of private banking control. It gave us the background against which there was such international banking effort to extend across the Atlantic similar privately owned and controlled central banking systems.

Paul Warburg, son of the prominent German banking family of M.M. Warburg & Company, and an officer of his father-in-law's international bank, Kuhn, Loeb and Company, spearheaded the efforts that resulted in the ultimate passage of the Federal Reserve Act.

President Wilson appointed Warburg to become a member of the first Federal Reserve Board and he served as both defender and sustainer of the central banking system he had been chiefly instrumental in foisting on this nation.

We quoted, from **Out of Debt, Out of Danger** by Jerry Voorhis, Congressman from California, and we quoted from **Money Creators** by Gertrude M. Coogan. Both books contain documented chronological coverage on the international efforts to burden this nation with a money supply based on interest bearing debt.

The credibility of Coogan's book is underscored by the fact that Senator Robert L. Owen, who was Chairman of the **Committee on Banking and Currency** of the United States Senate at the time of the secret meetings shaping the Federal Reserve Act, authenticated her research in his introduction to the book.

We noted Congressman Charles A. Lindbergh's heroic efforts to prevent the enactment of the Federal Reserve Act and quoted from his books **Banking and Currency and the Money Trust** and **Your Country at War.** He gave us clear insight into how the Money Trust had the nation in "bondage" and how it preferred "industrial slavery" to "chattel slavery".

Lindbergh's contribution to our thinking is important in two basic areas. First, private fractional reserve banking is not interested in merely foreclosing on homes, farms and businesses to acquire property per se. It is primarily interested in **exploiting** human effort and thus is constantly finding new borrowers who will accept interest-bearing loans and provide a continuous flow of unearned profits to the nation's usurers.

The second basic area is Lindbergh's awareness that inevitably there had to be a day when the "Money Trust" must give way to a "Public Trust" that included all the people. We quote:

> **Knowing these facts, will the people continue to remain in such a state of bondage? Certainly not! The trusts have taught us the principle of combination. If it is good and profitable for the trusts, it is good and profitable for the people. It would be better to have <u>one great trust created by all of the people for their common benefit</u> than to have our actions controlled by several trusts operated for the individual benefit of a few persons.**

Before we close this book we will be considering how the nation can have an honest banking system within the economic framework of a "public trust" or **National Cooperative Commonwealth.** We will grasp how the total work capability of the nation can be unleashed for an abundant and secure life for all the people.

We noted the Congressional Study (August, 1976) made public by the **Banking, Currency and Housing Committee** of the House of Representatives," chaired by Henry S. Reuss (D. Wisconsin). The Study bore out irrefutably the fact that the whole Federal Reserve System, including its 12 district banks, its branches, its member banks, and the Federal Reserve Board is an exclusive banker's fraternity operating in the interest **of** bankers, **for** bankers and **by** bankers.

Only two short paragraphs from the Study will suffice:

> **As the study makes clear, it is difficult to imagine a more narrowly-based board of directors for a public agency than has been gathered together for the twelve banks of the Federal Reserve System.**
>
> **Only two segments of American society, banking and big business, have any substantial representation on the boards, and often even these become merged through interlocking directorates.**

This Study dispelled the promoted myth that the Federal Reserve System is independent of corporate interests.

We focused on another Congressional hearing which is entitled: *Hearings before The Sub-Committee on Domestic Finance, of the Committee on Banking and Currency, House of Representatives, Eighty-eighth*

Congress, Second Session on the Federal Reserve System after Fifty Years, 3 vols. (1964)

Two publications, *"Primer on Money* and *"Money Facts"* were included in the Study.

There were many months of hearings in which the top personnel of not only the whole Federal Reserve System but dozens of experts from labor, past advisors to Presidents, authorities on law and political economy testified. The testimony was comprehensive and priceless in documenting the flawed operations of fractional-reserve banking during a fifty-year period.

We quoted extensively from the **Primer on Money** which well established how private banks part with nothing they possess in making loans to individuals, farmers or businesses. They monetize the borrower's assets or working capability. When the private banks create credit for the government, they receive United States interest-bearing bonds backed by the assets of the entire nation.

The private banking system by controlling the money supply, largely through the operations of the Open Market System, buying and selling government securities, it determines the amount of work the nation can do. More seriously, its continuous creation of loans, usually checkbook money, carries with the process a mushrooming interest debt of actually trillions of dollars.

The most revealing enlightenment coming out of all the questions and answers in the "Primer" is simply this: If the citizen's assets and working capability is sufficient for the private banks to create checkbook credit, and the government's bonds backed by the entire nation is sufficient to create public credit, why can't the **citizens and their government themselves create money and credit without any debt and without any interest?**

The obvious answer is loudly in the affirmative! All that is necessary is for the people to be informed as to the fallacy of private banking and the need to set up a debt-free and interest-free monetary system. As we have mentioned, it will be covered in closing chapters.

Vampiristic interest and mushrooming debt are evident throughout the whole functioning of the Federal Reserve System. Financial economists cite a total indebtedness, private and public, of over **30 trillion dollars.** And the total grows daily. As an unpayable debt, it is an unconscionable burden being placed on the unborn.

The Thomas Edison interview by **The New York Times** clearly demonstrated the unique difference between government bonds and government currency. His explanation was profound in its simplicity. We covered the interview quite lengthily and suffice it for now to quote two pertinent paragraphs:

> **It is absurd to say that our country can issue $30,000,000 in bonds and not $30,000,000 in currency. Both are promises to pay; but one promise fattens the usurer, the other helps the people. If the currency issued by the Government were no good, then the bonds issued would be no good either.**
>
> **If the United States Government will adopt this policy of increasing its wealth without contributing to the interest collector, for the whole national debt is made up of interest**

charges, then you will see an era of progress and prosperity in this country such as could never have come otherwise.

With the Summary fresh in our minds let us now focus on those individuals who challenged the nation's private banking system and those who offered proposals for the setting up of an honest system. . . .

24

"The greatest crime in history!"

THROUGHOUT our history courageous patriots have stood up to challenge the unconstitutionality of private control of the nation's money and credit. They recognized the needless suffering and economic injustice that was prevalent throughout the land caused by the debt-merchants who controlled the nation's monetary system.

They recognized that the most grievous crime against any people was tens of millions denied the very means of survival when at the same time there existed the work capability to provide an abundant and secure life for all the citizens of the society. Such socio-economic environment was unacceptable.

One of the most outstanding challengers to the Federal Reserve System was Congressman Louis T. McFadden.

Congressman Louis T. McFadden

IN A SPEECH on June 10, 1932 in the Congress of the United States, the Honorable Louis T. McFadden, Representative from Canton, Pennsylvania, made a speech that should go down in history with Patrick Henry's "Give me Liberty or give me Death!"

In this stirring speech he stated "The sacking of these United States by the Federal Reserve Board and the Federal Reserve Banks is **"the greatest crime in history!"**, and he presented documented facts to bear out his indictment. As we cite excerpts from his speech we should bear in mind that Congressman McFadden was the Chairman of the **House Committee on Banking and Currency.**

We should also be mindful of the fact that he delivered his speech when the nation had been thrown into the most devastating depression that the nation had ever endured. Some 15-20 million workers were out of jobs, and one third of the people were ill-clothed, ill-fed and ill-housed.

It was against this extremely dire economic condition that one can understand the harshness and righteous vehemence with which Congressman McFadden made his indictment of the Federal Reserve System. His memorable speech can be found in the Congressional Record, Page 12.983 for 1932.

We want to quote a number of paragraphs from his lengthy speech that ran to many pages:

> **Mr. Chairman, we have in this country one of the most corrupt institutions the world has ever known. I refer to the Federal Reserve Board and the Federal Reserve Banks. The Federal Reserve Board, a government board, has cheated the Government of these United States and the people of the United States out of enough money to pay the Nation's debt.**

> **The depredations and iniquities of the Federal Reserve Board and the Federal Reserve Banks acting together have cost this country enough money to pay the national debt several times over.**

> **This evil institution has impoverished and ruined the people of these United States, has bankrupt itself, and has practically bankrupted our government. It has done this through the**

152

defects of the law under which it operates, through the maladministration of that law by the Federal Reserve Board, and through the current practices of the moneyed vultures who control it.

Congressman McFadden emphatically clarified the mistaken myth that Federal Reserve Banks are the property of the United States Government. He stated:

Some people think the Federal Reserve Banks are United States Government institutions. They are private credit monopolies which prey upon the people of these United States for the benefit of themselves and their foreign customers; foreign and domestic speculators and swindlers; and rich and predatory money lenders.

These twelve private credit monopolies were deceitfully and disloyally foisted upon this country by bankers who came here from Europe and repaid us for our hospitality by undermining our American institutions.

President Wilson died a victim of deception. He had certain qualities of heart and mind, which entitled him to a high place in the councils of this nation, but he was not a banker. He admitted it. It was, therefore, on the advice of others that the iniquitous Federal Reserve Act, the death warrant of American liberty, became law in his administration.

Congressman McFadden felt strongly that it was the malfunctioning of our money and credit system and the colluding of the Federal Reserve Board and Federal Reserve Banks with "swindlers in all parts of the world" and "the riffraff of every country operating on the public credit of the United States Government" that led to the Great Depression of the 1930s.

He related to it with these words:

> Meanwhile and on account of it, we ourselves are in the midst of the greatest depression we have ever known. From the Atlantic to the Pacific, our country has been ravaged and laid waste by the evil practices of the Federal Reserve Board and the Federal Reserve Banks and the interests which control them. At no time in our history, has the general welfare of the people been at a lower level or the minds of the people so filled with despair.

> Recently, in one of States, 60,000 dwelling houses and farms were brought under the hammer in a single day; 71,000 houses and farms, in Oakland Country, Michigan, were sold and their erstwhile owners dispossessed. The people who have thus been driven out are the wastage of the Federal Reserve Act. They are the victims of the Federal Reserve Board and the Federal Reserve Banks.

One wonders how Congressman McFadden, now from a higher vantage point, views the current economic conditions in America nearly three-quarters of a century later. Certainly, he must view with incredulity, that the private banking system that he so courageously inveighed against was still in full power and the people were still tolerating its evils in causing wholesale bankruptcies, pervasive poverty throughout the land and millions futilely seeking jobs.

McFadden covered chronologically the steps leading up to the passage of the Federal Reserve Act, a repeat of what we have covered from other sources, and then followed up with the disastrous results of the the Federal Reserve System in action. One parallel circumstance was of particular interest having to do with large trade deficits.

Today, our nation is suffering a trade deficit of over 400 billion dollars and has had similar deficits for a number of years. Are the Federal Reserve Board and Federal Reserve Banks playing the same role today as they played during McFadden's time? This was his explanation:

> The United States has been ransacked and pillaged. Our structures have been gutted and only the walls are left standing. While this crime was being perpetrated, everything the world could rake up to sell us was brought in here at our own expense by the Federal Reserve Board and the Federal Reserve Banks until our markets were swamped with unneeded and un-wanted imported goods priced far above their value and thus made to equal the dollar volume of our honest exports, and to kill or reduce our favorable balance of trade.

> They act for their foreign principals and they accept fees from foreigners for acting against the best interests of these United States. Naturally there has been great competition among foreigners for the favors of the Federal Reserve Board.

Congressman McFadden's speech was quite long and since we will be noting his "Impeachment Resolution," which he introduced a year later, we will conclude his speech with a few of his closing remarks:

> The people of these United States are being greatly wronged. If they are not, then I do not

know what "wronging the people" means. They have been driven from their employments. They have been dispossessed of their homes. They have been evicted from their rented quarters. They have lost their children. They have been left to suffer and to die for lack of shelter, food, clothing and medicines.

The wealth of these United States and the working capital have been taken away from them and has either been locked in the vaults of certain banks and the great corporations or exported to foreign countries for the benefit of the foreign customers of these banks and corporations. So far as the people of these United States are concerned, the cupboard is bare.

The sack of these United States by the Federal Reserve Board and the Federal Reserve Banks is the greatest crime in history!

. . . The Federal Reserve Act should be repealed, and the Federal Reserve Banks, having violated their charters, should be liquidated immediately. Faithless government officers who have violated their oaths of office should be impeached and brought to trial.

Unless this is done by us, I predict, that the American people, outraged, pillaged, insulted and betrayed as they are in their own land, will rise in their wrath, and will sweep the money-changers out of the temple.

* * * * *

Just short of a year later, on May 23, 1933, Congressman Louis T. McFadden arose on the floor of the Congress and introduced an "Impeachment

156

Resolution" that not only included current members of the Federal Reserve Board and Federal Reserve Banks but past members as well. He made introductory remarks similar to what he had made in the speech from which you have just read excerpts.

One should read the whole lengthy Resolution to really do justice to what it embodies. However, just a few paragraphs will suffice to give you a sense of the seriousness and urgency of the Resolution:

> Whereas I charge them, jointly and severally, with violation of the Constitution and laws of the United States, with having taken funds from the United States Treasury which were not appropriated by the Congress of the United States, and I charge them with having unlawfully taken over $80,000,000,000 from the United States Government in the year 1928, the said unlawful taking consisting of the unlawful creation of claims against the United States Treasury to the extent of over $80,000,000,000 in the year 1928, and I charge them with similar thefts committed in 1929, 1930, 1931, 1932, and 1933, and in years previous to 1928, amounting to billions of dollars; and

> Whereas I charge them, jointly and severally, with having unlawfully created claims against the United States Treasury by unlawfully placing United States Government credit in specific amounts to the credit of foreign governments and foreign central banks of issue; private interests and commercial and private banks of the United States and foreign countries, and branches of foreign banks doing business in the United States, to the extent of billions of dollars; and with having made unlawful

157

contracts in the name of the United States Government and the United States Treasury; and having made false entries on books of account; and

Whereas I charge them, jointly and severally, with having brought about a repudiation of the national currency of the United States in order that the gold value of the said currency might be given to private interest, foreign governments, foreign central banks of issue, and the Bank for International Settlements, and the people of the United States be left without gold or lawful money and with no currency other than a paper currency irredeemable in gold, and I charge them with having done this for the benefit of private interests, foreign governments, foreign central banks of issue, and the Bank for International Settlements; and

Whereas I charge them, jointly and severally, with having reduced the United States from a first-class power to one that is dependent, and with having reduced the United States from a rich and powerful nation to one that is internationally poor; and

Whereas I charge them, jointly and severally, with the crime of having treasonably conspired and acted against the peace and security of the United States, and with having treasonably conspired to destroy constitutional government in the United States; Therefore be it

Resolved, That the Committee on the Judiciary is authorized and directed, as a whole or by subcommittee, to investigate the official conduct of Eugene Meyer, Roy A. Young, Edmund Platt, Eugene R. Black, Adolph Caspar Miller, Charles S. Hamlin, George R. James, Andrew W. Mellon,

Ogden L. Mills, William H. Woodin, John W. Pole, J. F. T. O'Conner, members of the Federal Reserve Board; and F. H. Curtiss, J. H. Case, R. L. Austin, George De Camp, L. B. Williams, W. W. Hoxton, Oscar Newton, E. M. Stevens, J. S. Wood, J. N. Payton, M. L. McClure, C. C. Walsh, Isaac B. Newton, Federal Reserve Agents, to determine whether, in the opinion of the said committee, they have been guilty of any high crime or misdemeanor which, the contemplation of the Constitution, requires the interposition of the constitutional powers of the House. Such committee shall report its findings to the House, together with such resolution or resolutions of impeachment or other recommendations, as it deems proper.

There were many other fundamental charges in the formal Resolution but from a layman's perspective they would be "overkill" and we feel that we have stated sufficient charges in McFadden's Impeachment Resolution for anyone to grasp the unconstitutional and criminal acts by those operating within the framework of the Federal Reserve System.

25

H. R. 17140

ON APRIL 23, 1970, the Honorable John R. Rarick rose in the House of Representatives and offered H. R. 17140 to "Restore confidence to our money through Constitutional Government." We are printing his remarks and his Resolution in full as they in much simpler terms, but equally profound, are a contrast to the meaty Impeachment Resolution of the Honorable Louis T. McFadden. It is interesting to note that it was nearly 40 years after McFadden's indictment of the Federal Reserve Board and the Federal Reserve banks that we have Congressman Rarick's remarks and Resolution:

> Mr. Speaker, the American people are bombarded with fearful reports on war, poverty, pollution, inflation, strikes, and violence, yet the foremost concern to every citizen is his money and its buying power.

> Because of this I have introduced H. R. 17140, a bill to vest in the Government of the United States the absolute, complete, and unconditional control of our money through Government ownership and control of the 12 Federal Reserve banks.

> I have taken this action because of an ever-increasing lack of public confidence in the private monopoly which presently is in charge of our money. Confidence and stability in our fiscal affairs could be restored by the Federal Reserve Board and private bankers but they refuse to discipline themselves voluntarily to meet the crisis they have precipitated.

Since the Federal Reserve bankers lack the responsibility to perform their duty, then Congress must concede that the Federal Reserve Act of 1913 has by experience proven itself a failure.

As one reads the following statistics on mushrooming indebtedness that so alarmed Congressman Rarick, give thought to the shattering alarm that he would have felt if he had been witness to the current burden of accumulated interest-bearing debt of **$32 trillion.** Rarick gave his assessment as of the year 1970:

When the Federal Reserve Act was signed into law in 1913, the U. S. public debt was $1 billion. As of January 1970 our national debt was $382 billion. The combined national debt, Federal, State, county, municipal, corporate and private, is fast approaching $2 trillion. The non-Federal debt is estimated at $1,347 billion. Farm debt at the end of 1969 has reached nearly $60 billion, up from $25 billion or almost doubled in the last 10 years.

We but owe it to ourselves is the response of the liberals to the figures. We owe it to someone but not to ourselves because we do not own our own money.

Consider that according to the Treasury report of January 1970 the total coinage in circulation was $5,965,000,000 and the total currency in circulation was $47,431,000,000. Yet of this evidence of wealth totaling $52,991,000,000 if $46,431,000,000 is Federal Reserve notes which belongs to the Federal Reserve then only $595,000,000 in currency belongs to our people or the Government. And this $46 billion of the Federal Reserve is lent into circulation by commercial banks for which credit on credit our people as borrowers pay interest.

Considering that the estimated interest on the national debt this year will exceed $18 billion, it must be apparent that this kind of credit lending has been a profitable institution, but not for our people of our country.

While Congressman Rarick was aware of a spiraling Federal indebtedness with accompanying interest, in his wildest extrapolation it is doubtful that he would have projected our current (2008) Federal indebtedness exceeding **9 trillion dollars** and interest charges hovering around **400 billion dollars** annually.

However, Congressman Rarick was on the mark in recognizing the consequences of unchecked debt on the economy. He graphically voiced his concerns:

Inflation and recession are destroying both the poor and the entrepreneur. Interest rates, already exceeding usury, give no sign of lowering and under expected economic law of supply and demand can be expected to soar higher. Unemployment increases stealthily. Most workers and producers are falsely led to believe the answer lies only in wage increases or price increases. The consumer seeks relief through price controls.

And behind the scenes our academic economists fumble to "think tank" sophisticated solutions to a problem they are unable to understand because it's beneath their comprehension. And any of the many proposals of the controlled intellectuals in the service of the cabal can but be temporal and could only worsen the problem by extending the time of any solution.

162

Before introducing H. R. 17140 Congressman Rarick stated without reservation his indictment of the Federal Reserve Act:

The Federal Reserve exclusive franchise was a mistake. Congress in 1913 erred tragically when it impudently delegated full control over our money to the Federal Reserve moneychangers, a private banking cartel. The act may carry defacto legality but no informed individual can deny its unconstitutionality and unjust powers over the money of our people.

Yet fear pervades our land and those who know the truth and could act are relegated to silence because someone's political future may be threatened or a friend embarrassed. My only comment is that unless we corral this monster in our midst the very Republic which includes not only the wealth but the intellect will be demolished.

We walk by faith and not by sight. Should confidence fail or falter the mightiest will fall first.

My bill H. R. 17140 provides the only viable and effective solution to the breakdown in confidence of our money and financial system. It is very simple. That we return the banks of the Federal Reserve System and full control over our money to the Congress. I claim no pride in authorship because this is and was intended by the Founding Fathers which they provided in the US Constitution, the law of the land:

The Congress shall have the power "to coin money, regulate the value thereof, and of foreign coin, and fix the standard of weights and measures." (Article 1, Section 8, clause 5)

163

Who should the people trust more than their Congress? If they disapprove we can be eliminated at the polls. Unelected bureaucrats and monopolistic bankers, never.

We of this House are the sole representatives of the American people. Our system is not a democracy because we are the only elected officials in the federal system. The Founding Fathers intended that the power to issue and control money was only to be entrusted to the hands of those elected officials who are constantly accountable to the voters.

H. R. 17140

Be it enacted by the Senate and House of Representatives of the United States of America in Congress assembled, that

(a) the Secretary of the Treasury of the United States is hereby authorized and directed "forthwith to purchase the capital stock of the twelve Federal Reserve Banks and branches and agencies thereof, and to pay to the owners thereof the par value of such stock at the date of purchase."

(b) All member banks of the Federal Reserve System are hereby required and directed to deliver forthwith to the Treasurer of the United States, by the execution and delivery of such document as may be prescribed by the Secretary of the Treasury, all the stock of such Federal Reserve banks owned or controlled by them, together with all claims of any kind or nature in and to the capital assets of the said Federal Reserve banks, it being the intention of this Act to vest in the Government of the United States the

absolute, complete, and unconditional ownership of the said Federal Reserve banks.

(c) There is hereby authorized to be appropriated, out of any funds not otherwise
appropriated, such sums as may be necessary
to carry out the purposes of this Act.

* * * * *

As anticipated, Congressman Rarick's Resolution
suffered the same fate as the Impeachment Resolution
of Congressman Louis T. McFadden. Neither the
Congress nor a sufficiently enlightened electorate were
ready to confront "the greatest crime in history".

Sporadically, Congressmen like Wright Patman of
Texas, T. Allan Goldsborough of Maryland and others
have introduced Bills or Resolutions to give Congress
the constitutional control of the nation's money and
credit. They sought changes in the Federal Reserve Act
and demanded an accounting of the operations of the
Federal Reserve Board and the Federal Reserve Banks.

In any tangible sense, all were futile efforts.

Today, we are a nation stumbling without insight or
purposeful goal. We are truly a nation of the blind
leading the blind. A financial monster occupies our
land exploiting our labor and is insensitive to the tens
of millions in want. To date there has been no hand to
stay the oppressive and cruel operations of the lending
institutions of the nation.

A suffering people want a better society. They want a
chance to have constant work to provide food and
shelter for their loved ones. They want a secure home
free from threats of foreclosure and bureaucratic taxes.
They want available to them all needed services of

165

health care, both medical and preventive, in times of sickness or injury.

They want their rivers, lakes, waterways, soil and air free of contaminants. Especially they want the absence of both low and high radioactive material threatening their lives and the fate of the earth itself.

They want their children to have full opportunity at education without being saddled with tens of thousands in debt as they leave college.

They want an end to their sons, daughters, mothers and fathers being sent to die in undefined and needless wars. They want a society that believes in the importance and the preciousness of every life, irrespective of race, color, religion, nationality or life-orientation.

Most of all, they want the kind of a society that is peaceful, honest and equitable to be passed on to the unborn.

Clearly, it must penetrate the minds of all perceptive citizens that these hopes and dreams cannot become a reality until the "money changers are driven out of the temple."

Against the background of all that we have presented, and will present, respecting private banking, corporate control of the economy and a captive Congress, the balance of this book will deal with the three areas: **Enlightenment, Proposals** and **Action.**

Enlightenment: Only with a basic understanding of the barriers or flaws in our way of caring on the nation's business can there be the prerequisite understanding needed to propose solutions.

Proposals: These are the actual solutions that will eliminate the barriers and flaws unleashing the full work capability of the society for an equitable and abundant society.

Action: Uncompromising and unflinching effort is required. to achieve the endorsement and adoption of the proposals.

President Lincoln's Springfield speech at the Republican State Convention, June 16, 1858 states succinctly our challenge in meeting today's crisis:

> **If we could first know where we are, and whither we are tending, we could better judge what to do, and how to do it. We are now far into the fifth year since a policy was initiated with the avowed object and confident promise of putting an end to slavery agitation. Under the operation of that policy, that agitation has not only not ceased but has constantly augmented. In my opinion, it will not cease until a crisis shall have been reached and passed. "A house divided against itself cannot stand!"**

Certainly, where we are and "whither we are tending" are prerequisites for challenging the ills of the nation!

~ 26 ~
Enlightenment

INFORMATION IS POWER and those who own and control the nation's media have the instruments in their hands to enslave a people economically, financially and politically. Today, there is over-whelming evidence as to the concentrated corporate ownership of radio, TV, cable, Internet and all the areas of print. What the citizenry see, what they hear and what they read are at the absolute control of **six corporate conglomerates.**

From the very inception of this nation it has been fundamental to the thinking of those seeking constitutional revolutionary change that an **informed citizenry** is imperative. As we have stated, there must be a clear understanding as to the economic and political barriers preventing an equitable and democratic society. And, there must be a clear understanding as to the solutions that would surmount those barriers.

In short, there must be a irrefutable grasp as to the forces entrenched in power that exploit and enslave the citizenry. And, in turn, there must be a clear understanding of the proposals that would unseat usurped power and allow for the unleashing of the nation's full productive capability for a fair, abundant life for all the people.

Clearly, monopolistic corporate power is not concerned over protest per se. In fact, to a large extent they welcome it. It allows the oppressed citizenry to vent their righteous feelings without posing any challenge to those in power. However, at the same time, it must be recognized that aggressive, constructive protest does serve effectively in underscoring the nature of the serious problems besetting the nation.

The broad enlightenment that must come to the people is to understand the four basic flaws of our private capitalist system. We will deal with them separately:

No restraints on the growth of unnatural entities, corporations.

DURING THE PAST century there is a historical record of progressive corporate takeover of the economy. However, it has been the past twenty years that we have been witness to a mania of mergers creating larger and larger corporate conglomerates owning and controlling every segment of the nation's business.

Hundreds of thousands of small and medium-sized enterprises have ruthlessly been driven out of the economy. The anti-trust laws (both the Sherman and Clayton Acts) have politically been rendered helpless to enforce the "restraint on trade" and the "monopolistic prohibitions" of the Acts.

Corporate fraud, manipulation of books and CEO unconscionable greed, along with destruction of pension funds and the tragedy of the "downsizing" of millions of the best jobs are constantly in the news. CNN has a daily tally (2004) of the hundreds of CEOs charged with criminal practices and since the collapse of Enron few persons have been sent to jail.

The foregoing focuses on the dire consequences of corporate despotic abuse but does not focus on the

169

hidden inherent injustice of our economic dilemma. In the minds of the people must arise this compelling question. How come that the nation's workers, consumers and taxpayers, did not get their **proportionate ownership** of the national corporate work capability that they helped build?

Inescapable is the circumstance of the workers giving their sweat and blood for unfair wages with their effort redounding solely to the corporate owners. Equally evident is the role of the consumers who paid "fixed prices" with the unearned profits redounding solely to the corporate owners. And, as taxpayers their taxes underwrote the government subsidized R&D (research and development), which redounded solely to the corporations.

Less than 5% of the nation's families own the major stock in the nation's total industrial plant and the vast majority of the citizenry having neither stock ownership nor dividend claims against the products and services which their labor made possible.

If the workers, consumers and taxpayers had received their **proportionate equity**, along with management, they, too, could have received dividends like the affluent and privileged, and enjoyed purchasing claims against the goods and services, especially at times of unemployment.

"Unnatural" Corporate Power versus the "natural rights" of the people

SINCE THE INCEPTION of the nation, there has been a constant struggle between citizens, as "natural" entities, versus corporations as "unnatural" entities. There has been a constant battle by the people to eliminate corporate abusive behavior by denying corporations "personhood" status.

With the adoption of the 14th Amendment to the Constitution corporate interests began a concerted legal drive to have themselves protected by the "protection clause" that applied to the black citizens. They saw the terrific advantage that they would have if property were given human status and "no person can be deprived of life, liberty or property without due process."

An article appearing **In These Times,** February 8, 1998, by Joel Bleifuss, covers a brief history of corporations particularly in respect to Supreme Court decisions. The most definitive Supreme Court decision was the *Santa Clara County v. Southern Pacific Railroad* in which corporate lawyers achieved their goal with the Supreme Court declaring that the 14th Amendment applied to corporations.

Bleifuss in his article stated:

> **Although courts now permit government regulation of business, corporations have managed to retain the First Amendment rights they were given in** *Santa Clara.* **Few, if any, mainstream voices consider the question: Should corporations have the same rights as people have? Corporations based in the United States wield vast economic and political power. They can live forever. They feel no pain. They do not need clean air to breathe, potable water to drink or healthy food to eat. Their only goal is to grow bigger and more powerful.**
>
> **Rather than treating these institutions as if they were flesh and blood, the political and legal system should acknowledge the fact that cor-**

porations are merely one way that people organize themselves to do business. They are not "endowed by the creator with unalienable rights" but rather are human-made creatures that can just as easily be unmade if they cease to serve a worthwhile public function

The foregoing must be foremost in the minds of the sovereign people in working out a just and abundant economic society. When we cover the chapter on "Proposals" we will learn how the stolen wealth of the nation can be restored to the people and how every person will have a purchasing claim against all goods and services along with a decision-making voice.

Most importantly, we will learn how a society can be created in which the young can have hope, inspiration and the opportunity to develop their inner potentials to the optimum.

~ 27 ~

Private banking control of the nation's money and credit

THIS IS THE SECOND major flaw in our private capitalist economic system. We have covered with much detail and documentation the history of our Federal Reserve System resulting in trillions of dollars in interest-bearing indebtedness, untold suffering and an inability of the nation to fund life-threatening human needs.

The most salient concept that the reader should grasp is the unmitigated deceit inherent in the functioning of the Federal Reserve System. It is simply this: The private banks create the nation's money and credit by **monetizing the citizen's assets and work capability and lend it to them in the form of interest-bearing debt.** The banks part with nothing that they themselves possess.

We documented the interlocking directorships between the largest banks and the largest non-financial corporations. We documented "vampiristic interest" and mushrooming indebtedness. We noted the criminal collusion between the banks and corrupt corporations. Let us single out one outstanding case.

The New York Times of July 29, 2003 carried this revealing disclosure. The two largest banks in the nation, **Citigroup** and **J. P. Morgan Chase**, agreed to pay 300 million dollars in fines and penalties to settle accusations that they aided Enron in misrepresenting its true financial conditions for years before the company collapsed.

Such criminal practices have been part and parcel throughout the private banking system.

Finally, let me quote from my book **A Blueprint for Survival,** starting on page 44, how banks fit into the mania of corporate mergers during the last quarter of the past century.

> With merger of Chase Manhattan and Chemical Bank in 1995, making it the largest bank at that time, with more than 300 billion dollars in assets, there has been an explosion in mergers. It was followed by Citigroup, Inc. and Bank-America with over 600 billion dollars in assets.
>
> The Federal Reserve Bank of Atlanta in its "Economic Review Fourth Quarter 1999" lists the mergers and acquisitions from 1989-99. During that ten-year period there were a total of 3,844 mergers with bank assets of $3,210,785,-000,000 (greater than 3 trillion!) and deposits of $2,279,563,000,000 (2 and ¼ trillion!).
>
> The Glass-Seagall Act adopted in 1933 effectively kept the commercial banks out of the mainstream of domestic investment banking. With the enactment of the Gramm-Leach-Bliley Act (1999), pressured for by the large commercial banks that can now cross state lines, swallow up small and medium-size banks and merge with the nation's largest insurance companies.
>
> No longer is there a personal relationship with the banks. Humans have become lifeless statistics on the bank's computers to be added, subtracted, discounted and deleted.

While there are not sufficient harsh words to indict the economic injustices and widespread oppression caused by the private banking institutions under the Federal Reserve System, one must conclude fairly that not all bankers, especially the employees of the banking business, are themselves dishonest or conscious destroyers of the public good.

Etched on our minds must be the recognition that it is the **private banking system itself** that calls for our severest condemnation and indictment.

We all live in an aberated society that is neither safe nor solvent and everyone, rich or poor, banker or non-banker, is equally a victim of an unworkable, unjust and archaic financial system irrespective of one's economic station in life.

It behooves all of us to act in concert in "driving the moneychangers out of the Temple" and bringing about constructive change in our lives!

~ 28 ~
Pattern for Political Slavery

THE THIRD flaw in our private capitalist system is the circumstance that those who control the economic and financial systems control the political processes by which government operates. In short, the formula for taking over any people is first to get control of a nation's issuance of money, then corral all of its industrial assets, and finally through these interlocking monopolies underwrite all major candidates who will be beholden to the wishes and dictates of their underwriters.

Over-simplified, this is a **pattern for political slavery**. Unfortunately, it is the fate that has befallen America.

(The basic thinking of this chapter is taken from my book **A Blueprint for Survival.)**

By and large, with few exceptions, the men and women who hold political office, on every level of government, are those who have been carefully screened by the economic and financial "establishments" that wield dominant power on every stratum of our society.

The electorate has had no meaningful role in their selection. It should not be difficult to realize that such selected political officeholders are not only lackeys of those who made their elections possible but at the same time have become entrapped themselves in defending economic injustice that their own political opportunism might be assured.

From the operating of the local license bureau to the appointments of postmasters, to the recommending of judgeships, to the awarding of hundreds of billions of tax dollars in public projects and weaponry contracts, all major political parties have employed and do employ **patronage** to perpetuate their existence through enforced political allegiance.

The November 15, 2000 issue of *"The Washington Spectator"* states, *"A new study by the non-partisan Center for Responsive Politics lists the financial contributions of, and in reality, the Congressional buying by, 120 industries and special-interest groups. It shows that over the ten years from 1990 to 2000 the top ten money manipulators gave a total of more than $7.5 billion to members of Congress."*

The result is that elected candidates are in the business of making political pay-offs, particularly in kowtowing to the dictates of corporate lobbyists and are not in the business of reflecting the rights and interests of the citizenry.

When such political compromise leads to not only blocking needed social change within our own borders but leads to the sending of America's finest young men and women to foreign soil, like Vietnam and Iraq, to die in the defense of the political and economic interests of multi-national corporations, then the whole political "game" is not only intolerable but is criminal

Observation of Senator Russell Long

On April 4, 1967 (a third of a century ago) Senator Russell Long, Majority Whip, rose on the floor of the Senate Chamber and voiced an analysis of the political process. What he had to say is as timely and relevant today as it was then:

> Because of the high cost of campaigning and the inability of most candidates to pay the cost themselves, every corporation, every vested interest, every monopoly, every businessman in America, particularly the large and wealthy ones, have virtual standing invitation to contribute large sums of money and in return to receive assurances of one sort or another that they will receive a sympathetic ear.

> Here is where the big corporations, acting through their executives, have the opportunity to gain assurance that interest rates will not be very low, that monopolies will not be upset radically, that appointees to regulatory agencies will be acceptable to those whom they are supposed to regulate, that the wealthy will continue to enjoy tax loopholes.

Senator Long capsulated clearly and succinctly the roles of wealth, monopolies, lobbyists and compromised candidates!

Political parties

THE WHOLE promotion of the "two-party" system concept is to trick the electorate into believing it has a choice in political leadership when in reality such acceptance is sheer deception. To hear the proponents and apologists defend such system, one would think that the whole idea had been delivered to this nation on tablets of gold by angelic messenger.

In fact, anyone brash enough to question its divine origin is quickly charged with blasphemy and promoting political anarchy. It is all a ruse to protect the usurpers of authority.

Of course, the defenders of the two major political parties contend that they make possible divergent points of view and thus the electorate has a choice in voting for candidates. Such theory is but a smokescreen blinding the people to the irrefutable fact that all major candidates are selected and promoted by the political parties who are but fronts for the corporate structures in the society.

Even on the local level, it is the "establishments" that exercise the prevailing political voice.

To the enlightened there is no more sickening demonstration in the sacred name of a "free society" than national political conventions. From the first sound of the gavel to the final swish of the janitor's broom, such conventions are an insult to any rational person. In sheer hypocrisy and sham, they have no equal. What is disturbing, of course, is the fact that they represent the political mechanics by which are chosen the individuals to hold the highest offices in our government.

Political conventions! Let us recognize them for the subterfuge they are. They are the modern day replica of the Roman Circus. Behind all the trappings, the hoopla and discordant sound, the histrionics of arm-waving and patriotic vaporings, the confusion and the milling of delegates, behind all these is the feeding of the American electorate to the lions of political intrigue and double-cross. . . .

Government of lobbyists, by lobbyists and for lobbyists

IT IS ESTIMTED that there are 80,000 lobbyists in Washington who spend upwards of one billion dollars a year to protect and advance legislation in behalf of their corporate employers who pay them lush salaries. Many are "revolving door" members of Congress who know the ins and outs of Washington and become indispensble "buddies" with newly elected members.

Because lobbyists have unlimited money at their disposal, they become the foot soldiers for Congress, and the Executive Branch, and not only do the research but actually write much of the legislation that members haven't the time or disposition to do. This gives them constant access and with access comes constant influence.

The setting up of phone banks in Washington, and in other cities, to pressure members of Congress in support of privileged legislation is all part of the contrived elections.

Organizations like "The Business Roundtable," "The U. S. Chamber of Commerce," "The National Manufacturers Association," "The American Bankers Association" and "The American Medical Association" have memberships that include the financial and non-financial CEOs of the nation. Their political clout is constantly exercised in the Halls of State.

Finally, it is monopolistic ownership and control of the nation's media that subverts the whole process of election and legislation. In 1983 news monopolists numbered 50. Today, according to Ben Bagdikian, veteran news media critic, in his book **The Media**

Monopoly (2000) a mere 6 conglomerates have monopolistic control over all the outlets---newspapers, magazines, radio, television and Internet---and the numbers are shrinking.

Illegally raising campaign money via the ruse of "soft money" hundreds of millions of dollars are spent via newspapers, radio and TV to convey distorted information to create public opinion and influence elections. Candidates are portrayed favorably or unfavorably based on their willingness to do the **bidding** of the major political parties.

CNN covered the release on February 5, 2001 of a landmark study by Brigham Young University that concluded that political parties spent $400 million in soft money in the election year of 2000!

Proportionate representation

THE QUESTION OF VOTER representation itself discloses an over-all conceptual flaw in the outcome of elections. Consider the fact that if 51 percent of those who vote elect the winner candidate, the other 49 percent who voted for the loser candidate have no representation if the two candidates had diametrically opposing views.

And an even more serious development occurs when an independent, or third, candidate is added to the ballot of the two major parties. Should two of the candidates get 30 percent each of the votes, that leaves only 40 percent for the winner who now is elected and vouched for by less than a majority of the voters. And this takes place when less than 50 percent of all registered voters even bother to vote!

The absence of proportionate representation could be conceptually the most serious flaw in the elective structure. It is unacceptable that tens of millions seeking justice for specific problems in farming, in labor, in environment, in education or medical care are given no representation because their candidate got less votes. Such flagrant denial of legislative voice is in essence disenfranchisement.

Electoral College

THE SAME disenfranchisement occurs in the election of the highest offices in the land, president and vice-president, when the Electoral College can override the popular vote. What happened in Florida in 2000 should have dismayed and disenchanted all voters throughout the land as to the existing process by which they elect their leaders. For weeks the whole process was in limbo and the final decision witnessed the highest court in Florida and the nation's Supreme Court bowing to partisan politics.

The dissent by Supreme Court Justice John Paul Stevens in the *Bush v. Gore* Florida recount case best expresses in a few succinct words the heart of the elective debacle:

> **Although we may never know with complete certainty the identity of the winner of this year's presidential election, the identity of the loser is perfectly clear. It is the nation's confidence in the judge as any impartial guardian of the rule of law.**

No need to belabor the election fiasco further!

Democracy

NO WORD is employed as frequently in denoting our form of government and in defining our elective and political processes as the word "democracy". How is it defined in any respectable dictionary? It is defined clearly and simply **as rule of and by the authority of the people.**

In light of what we have just covered as to how the whole political process is permeated with pay-offs, PACs, media distortion, or underwritten by hundreds of millions in "soft money", no proportionate representation, government **of** lobbyists, **by** lobbyists and **for** lobbyists, partisan judges and less than 50 percent of the electorate even voting, how hypocritical and brazen to even suggest that we are a democracy!

The voters are pawns in the whole process and play no meaningful role in either elections or legislation. Political candidates are beholden to those who underwrite their campaigns and the political parties themselves serve as buffers between the electorate and their government.

When we come to consider political rule of and by the "authority of the people" in an upcoming chapter dealing with **Proposals** we will understand the guidelines that will give the people absolute sovereignty for the first time in the whole political process. . . .

~ 29 ~
Taming of Science and Technology

THE FOURTH and final basic structural flaw in our private capitalist system is the **inability of the social-economic-financial system to constructively accommodate the advancements in science and technology.** It has been a two-edged sword with strides made in many fields of human endeavor but at the same time it has failed to meet the needs of tens of millions of citizens faced with serious threats to life itself.

Since very earliest history, when a strong back, elementary tools and a pioneering spirit made up work capability, there has been a progressive application of science to the whole spectrum of life. From the first application of power, to the introduction of the assembly line, to automation and cybernation, and finally computerization, this nation has been witness to a progressive explosion in manufacturing, transportation, communication, and in all the other complementing and related areas.

In 1961, a Sub-Committee of the House of Representatives, chaired by Representative Holland, conducted in-depth hearings on the "Impact of Automation on Employment." Based on the testimony of the most knowledgeable people in all the scientific and technical fields involved in the subject, the Committee concluded that at that time, employing its best work capability, all the nation's services and products, including all that was shipped abroad, could be produced with only ten percent the total work force.

At that time, 40 years ago, the technological potential existed so that every worker would have been required to work only a four-hour week if the nation's technology were employed fully and constructively. However, the private capitalistic system, flawly structured, and driven by insatiable corporate greed, could not accommodate advancing science and applicable technology.

The same, of course, is graphically true today as we witness major "downsizing" not only on the assembly line and in managerial positions but throughout every segment of the economy.

The flaw, a cardinal flaw, in the whole relationship of workers, consumers and taxpayers to production is that the CEOs, and the major stockholders at the top, got exclusive ownership of the "national productive plant" and the **people got no equity.** If the people had gotten their rightful proportionate ownership then they would have had purchasing power by stock-dividends.

Destroyed purchasing power forces the corporate owners to resort to built-in obsolescence and the displaced workers are forced to go into debt to make up for the lost buying power. The whole process is a vicious cycle.

Clearly, the private capitalist system does not allow for the full utilization of a nation's advancing technology and work potential. That is why, when we are over-awed by the progress, technologically, that the nation has made in refrigeration, communications, transportation, electrical appliances of all kinds, productive techniques as in agriculture and even miraculous strides in medicine, we should realize that far, far greater and safer strides could have been made if technical know-how would have been fully employed constructively.

In terms of the millions of children who have been warped in body and mind, or died, who could have been properly fed; in terms of the boys and girls who could have been educated; in terms of the decent homes, safe cars, adequate hospitals that could have been constructed; in terms of universal preventive and medical treatment; in terms of repair and replacement of the entire infra-structure; and in terms of unpolluted water, air and soil, our technological work capability has only been **partially** employed.

The most serious indictment against the private capitalist system is that there have existed serious **unmet human needs** while at the same time there has been **unused technologic work capability** to fulfill those needs!

Super-highway of Information

MUCH IS MADE of the democratic potential of computerized technology, of the Internet and the super-highway of information.. It is stressed, as it was likewise stressed with past advances of communication, particularly the radio and television, that once again there would be a major step in the broadening and functioning of democracy. This, of course, has not happened.

In fact, there has been a lessening of democracy. Not only has there been less and less voter turnout but wider access to the people has only permitted those who control all areas of the media **to increase the volume of misinformation.**

With the initial introduction of the computer, the criteria "garbage-in, garbage-out" was highlighted as the operating equation for judging its quality and effectiveness. That was the best yardstick then and it is the best yardstick now. Along with the political area, computerization applies to all areas, including seductive advertising and corporate encroachment into education.

Break-through via Carnage

A SOBERING thought to consider is that the major break-throughs in technology have come about because wars have unleashed our productive energies. In the purported name of "national security" exorbitant taxes have been made acceptable and the people have supinely tolerated a state of servitude to overlording government and perpetual bondage.

The most nightmarish circumstance, and misuse of technology, has been in the field of nuclear weaponry. It poses the day-to-day prospect of a nuclear war, a "nuclear winter" and the obliteration of all life. It is estimated that some 30,000 missiles with nuclear warheads exist with the overwhelming number held by Russia and the United States.

While we have refused to sign the "Nuclear Non-proliferation Treaty" we threaten war when smaller nation's want a nuclear capability for their own defense. The same contradictory position maintains in reference to chemical and biological weapons. And, what about our refusal to join with other nations in banning "field mines" that are killing thousands of innocent victims?

We are blind to the fact that we were the first nation in the world to use atomic bombs. And we conveniently forget that we dumped over 13,000,000 gallons of the deadly chemical "agent orange" in an indiscriminate defoliage onslaught on the Vietnamese with tens of thousands dying agonizing deaths from untreated burns.

We have adopted the position that the powerful have the selective right to do what they want simply because they reign supreme in technology and military might.

Multinational globalization and a military doctrine of "unilateral preemptive strike" against any nation that challenges corporate predatory domination, foredooms a world to unchecked terrorism, violence and anarchy!

How tragic that tens of thousands of our finest men and women have paid, and still pay, the highest sacrifice in perpetual cold and hot wars to keep unworkable economic, financial and political systems afloat!

~ 30 ~

Proposals

WE NOW COME to consider the most important chapters in this book, the blueprinted solutions to our national dilemma and the action necessary to actualize those solutions. Our major effort to this point has been to focus on the private banking structure of the nation and how it in conjunction with our structurally flawed economic, financial and political systems have left our nation devastated economically and politically.

We have stressed that our economic, financial political systems must be restructured to bring about fairness and economic stability in our lives. We have also stressed that the primary culpability does not rest with the personnel who have functioned within those systems, however abusive their behavior, but rests with the **systems themselves.**

It is a waste of time and effort to be hypnotically focused on individuals who function within flawed economic, financial and political systems when upon their dismissal, or even indictment, a new set of personnel arises to take their place. The faulty systems continue to cause their harm and injustice.

It is within the context of the whole society that we must give direct consideration to the restructuring of our unconstitutional privately-owned and controlled banking structure placing the people and their government in perpetual bondage. And then we must, in the context of the whole society, give consideration to the restructuring of the private capitalist "free enterprise" and "open market" framework itself which has encouraged and allowed monopolistic abusive corporate power.

Efforts in the Past

THERE HAVE BEEN many outstanding individuals and organizations that have advanced proposals for national economic, financial and political change in this nation. While their efforts were not all inclusive in total renovation of the nation, the worth of their efforts should not be minimized.

The important fact is that their efforts contributed in educating the people as to fundamental wrongs and steps that would better their economic status. The most unique feature of all such effort, in contrast to most efforts today, was that the people were given programs that they could be for instead of the ultimate futile effort of just being against injustice and political corruption.

Outstanding in effort was Edward Bellamy, writer and political activist, who at the end of the 19th Century advanced the proposal for "A National Industrial State". In his book **Equality** he scathingly critiques the unworkability and abuses of Private Capitalism and presents an equitable economic framework for conducting the nation's business.

During that same general period, with stringent economic conditions of unemployment and foreclosures, and the emergence of the whole spectrum of "Robber Barons", the conditions were fertile for the rise of the "Populist Movement." One of the organizations that came into prominence at that time was the **Farmers Alliance.** Populist Charles W. McCune, a Texas Alliance leader, proposed his "Sub-treasury Plan" which was unique in creating agricultural capital based on real wealth, the farmer's own production.

It was during the Great Depression of the 1930s that there was a plethora of national proposals for dealing with the severe economic pressures of that period. As during the latter part of the Nineteenth Century, it was poverty, joblessness, indebtedness and foreclosures that prompted rethinking of the causes of the nation's dilemma and what could be done to relieve the situation..

On the West Coast, Upton Sinclair organized behind the slogan of "Ham and Eggs." Senator Huey Long of Louisiana was exhorting the people that "Every Man a King" was a realistic goal. Father Coughlin, the feisty and learned priest of Michigan, decried and exposed the evils of private banking via radio and published his monthly magazine **"Social Justice."**

Ralph Townsend founded "**The Townsend Plan** and crossed the depth and breadth of the nation organizing and calling for a special government stipend for the elderly to increase purchasing power and jump-start the whole economy. Tens of thousands rallied to his proposal.

Across our borders a Scottish engineer, Clifford Hugh Douglas, founded **"Social Credit"** which took on real momentum. Even today there are real adherents to his proposals. Its economic premise is logical and on the right track. The Canadian Treasury would provide "social credits" which would supplement existing purchasing power so the nation's consumers could acquire the goods and services that had been produced and were available for purchase.

Those unfamiliar with the proposals of "Social Credit" "and its background should subscribe to **Michael's Journal,** a Canadian publication which comprehensively and clearly explains the economic plan in conjunction with restoring to the government the issuance of the nation's credit and money.

The foregoing efforts, only briefly covered, were not successful in achieving sufficient popular support, but they contributed effectively in educating the people as to fundamental wrongs and steps that would better their economic status.

They were purposely selected because they gave the people something to be for instead of just being against perceived wrongs.

31

A Sense of Direction

I HAVE CHOSEN to focus primarily on a proposal called a **National Cooperative Commonwealth** because it uncannily solves the private banking behemoth and at the same time gives us an economic-political framework within which to carry on the total business of the nation and achieve the optimum well-being of the total citizenry.

In both these roles the "Commonwealth Idea" is the most inclusive solution for our consideration and understanding. The Idea was outlined in a book called **No More Hunger** by William Dudley Pelley during the heart of the Great Depression of the 1930s.

One feels an accelerating uplift and satisfaction when first getting acquainted with the Commonwealth Idea. It is as if a light had suddenly been turned on, or a compass had been dropped into the hands of one lost in the wilderness, or a lifesaver had been tossed to one helplessly drowning. A sense of direction presents itself with full impact. And what is the import of that sense of direction? It is this:

If the corporate structure has worked so successfully as a business framework for the few, what is to prevent the adoption of that same framework for operating a successful national business creating the good life for the entire 300,000,000 people in this nation?

In short, why not incorporate the entire economy into a **National Corporate Commonwealth** in which **every** human being would be both a common

193

stockholder and a preferred stockholder? Thus, every citizen would not only have a voice in shaping his economic life but at the same time every citizen would be a dividend-receiving stockholder giving him or her perpetual and inviolate purchasing claim against the full productive capability of the nation.

As such participant, every person would have a **stake** within the nation but more importantly he or she would have an **ownership** in the nation. The "maximization of profit," or more appropriately, the maximization of effort, would redound to all the people.

Certainly, if it is acceptable for powerful industrial and financial multinational monopolies to use the **principle of incorporation** to concentrate the nation's natural resources and technological know-how in the hands of the predatory few, then the sovereign people have an even greater right to use the same principle for equitably and justly making the good life a reality for each and every citizen.

Instead, of the few being capitalists, every human being would be a capitalist. Instead of private capitalism, we would have public capitalism. Instead of one giant transnational corporate **conglomerate**, a ominous condition that looms on the horizon, we would have a **National Cooperative Commonwealth.**

Its strength and integrity would be inherent in the people owning and coordinating their total work capability.

Planned Economy

AN INITIAL REACTION, largely emotional, to the tenets of a National Cooperative Commonwealth is that it provides for a "planned economy". It seems that one can speak of any undertaking, personal or public, that deals with plans or designs and it is readily accepted as an intelligent approach to minimize effort and maximize results.

But, the moment one suggests the equally reasonable approach to the conducting of the nation's business it is spontaneously indicted as being regimentary and downright subversive.

How has such inconsistency crept into the average person's thinking? Why does he or she see red, communist-tinged red, the moment that one points out that the nation is stumbling along without a sense of constructive direction and one suggests that workable design and planning are imperatives?

One objective that immediately arises is that economic planning of any kind violates the concept of "free enterprise" and our whole free-market economy is jeopardized. Another reaction that comes to the fore is the prospect of an overlording bureaucracy dictating the movements and actions of every citizen.

Both reactions are momentarily understandable. Both are without substance.

There is nothing profound or technical about either the words "free" or "enterprise". One simply means doing things without restraint and the other simply means performing an act or operation. When one grasps the workings of an incorporated national economy one clearly realizes that its central purpose is to lift all

195

restraints so that the nation can do all those things that need to be done, and can be done.

It is giving reality to the premise of "free enterprise".

In its most elementary terms a National Cooperative Commonwealth is an economic framework within which the sovereign citizens themselves **direct** and **coordinate** all the nation's resources, raw stock, tools and technological know-how so that all the people can enjoy the maximum good life commensurate with the utilization of the nation's full productive potential. It is nothing more nor nothing less..

Outside of the earliest history of this nation, there has never truly been an economy of free enterprise. Private capitalism, coupled with private banking, has simply employed the idealistic phrase to cover up the compounding restraints it has imposed on the economy. All the gimmicks and instruments of **unearned profit** as reflected in fictitious bank credit, exorbitant interest, and the whole spectrum of monopolistic arbitrary price-fixing have been nothing but **camouflaged theft.**

The economic history of the nation has been a consistent pattern of the majority of the citizens being systematically short-suited of their rightful equity and purchasing power, and the voracious and power-mad pyramiding their ownership of the nation's natural resources and productive machinery. Along with progressively increased economic power came equally abnormal political power with all its privileged legislation and government's failure to enforce the nation's anti-trust laws.

The tens of millions of workers, consumers and taxpayers in this nation have become the robot slaves of an economic, financial and social system that has thrived on exploitation and imposed inequities. Private Capitalism has created the vacuums into which expanding bureaucracy, expanding state welfarism and expanding indebtedness have been foisted on the people to make up for the "system's" inefficiencies.

In contrast to European feudalism it is more dastardly and devious because the serfs of that distant day knew they were slaves and today the majority of the people are unaware of their slavery.

Nothing tugs so empathetically at the heartstrings of the enlightened than the realization that people endure suffering and injustice when all the time they have the power in their own hands to terminate both oppressive conditions. In this context the people themselves are their own worst enemy.

They could be secure, their needs could be abundantly met, political sovereignty could really be theirs, and all within a peaceful environment, if they would comprehend that the major problems are all **man-made** and as such they can all be solved with **man-made** solutions.

This is the central message that must be gotten across to the people. Once the people are aroused to give in-depth thought to the causes of their dilemma and plight, and especially to their inherent power to effect every change that will improve their lot, they will recognize the wisdom of adopting a **National Cooperative Commonwealth.**

32

"This Land is our land"

MANY PEOPLE in hearing for the first time about incorporating the entire economy will allow that it sounds quite feasible. Quickly, however, they will question how it can be brought into being. Persons so reacting are of course unaware of the present accelerated trend of multi-billion dollar mergers with less than two hundred industrial-financial corporate conglomerates owning and controlling the entire economy.

The trend of larger and larger corporate mergers is unmistakable and clear. The ultimate projection of one Super Corporate Giant with dominant power over the lives of the entire citizenry is an extrapolated stark reality. It is no longer a question of whether it is possible to incorporate the entire economy. It is only a question **who owns** the national corporation and **who benefits** from it!

Before we outline the actual structure of a "National Cooperative Commonwealth" we should spell out the people's initial proportionate claim to the nation's full productive capacity and then deal with retrieving that part which has been unjustly taken away from the people.

It is wishful thinking to believe that the rightful needs and happiness of the people can be achieved without restoring to the people full access to the nation's productive capability. The plight of the nation's workers, consumers and taxpayers is that they have settled for tokenism instead of demanding their rightful share which would have allowed them to create an equitable prosperous society.

Natural Heritage

THERE IS no difficulty in establishing that every person, even the most destitute, has an inherent right to the world's natural resources. The Creator did not departmentalize this earth, or our nation, designating who should have access to the abundance of raw stock, the unlimited levels of energy, including the airways. Every newborn child has an inherent right to the Bounty of Nature.

No individual or group has a right to build fences around the natural wealth of this nation and then say to the deprived millions born in this generation, "You have simply been born at a time when the land and the natural assets of the nation are not up for grabs."

The same reasoning must be applied to all the contributions that all the people have made to all knowledge up the many centuries. Such contributions are not the exclusive knowledge of the few to enhance only their own well-being and survival. All achievements, and all advancements, up the corridors of time in physics, in chemistry, in transportation, in communication, in the techniques of production, in medicine, are the legacy of all the people.

It is immaterial whether you have, or do not have, a scientific grasp of what the Galileos, the Keplers, and the Newtons contributed to the first understanding of heavenly bodies and the forces of nature. It is not necessary that you understand what the James Watts contributed to the first application of power to machines, what the Marconis, the Faradays, the Maxwells and the Edisons contributed to an understanding and application of electricity.

Nor do you have to grasp the exhaustive and painstaking research and experimentation that encompasses all the contributions of the Bohrs, the Daltons, the Einsteins, and the Enrico Fermis from the first detection of atomic structure up to the present harnessing of nuclear power.

There would be no end to our listings if we were to cover the contributions of the first alphabet, the first offerings in mathematics, the first steps in metallurgy, the first crude machines of farm, of factory and of transportation, the first movable type and the steps toward wireless communication, the first discoveries in medicine, and the firsts in every existing field of human endeavor, and then trace them to the present.

Included, of course, would have to be the millions, the billions, of people themselves who have inhabited the planet. Without their contributions, however menial, all achievements in science, technology, and in the clearing, the cultivating and the building of the world would have been impossible.

Each person now living has a stake in all that learned men have contributed and sacrificed up the centuries. Our present know-how is but an extension of all the genius and labor that preceded those living today.

Every person has an inherent stake in the material and energy makeup of the world, including accumulated knowledge, simply because he or she is born!

~ 33 ~
Retrieving the People's Wealth

IT MUST BE FIRST recognized that since the founding of this nation, it has been the contributions of the total people, as workers, consumers and taxpayers, who have directly and indirectly made possible the existence and expansion of all the resultant monopolies in both goods and services. Neither the people's effort, nor their inherent claim to natural resources, have been recognized and rightfully accredited.

As we have stated repeatedly, the most economic injustice that has maintained up the generations is that the people were not given their **proportionate ownership** of that which they made possible through their effort.

It is against the foregoing background that the sovereign people must square their shoulders and with determined conviction declare loud and clear that the **current ownership and control** of the nation's natural resources and productive capability are not a **valid ownership and control.**

"We the People" declare that within the "equal protection clauses" of both the Fifth and Fourteenth Amendments of the Constitution we **have been deprived of** "life, liberty and property without due process" and we have the constitutional power to retrieve that, which has been illegally taken from us

We want peace with economic justice!

We demand peace with economic justice!

There are three major legal steps that can be taken to retrieve the people's rightful assets:

1. **The taxing power of government.** This power implemented with price controls and the closing of tax loopholes, could force the multi-billion-dollar corporate conglomerates to return to the entire citizenry the hundreds of dollars, actually trillions of dollars, in assets that were made possible by the nation's workers, consumers and taxpayers.

In essence the monopolies of industry and services by the whole gamut of "price-fixing", extracting unearned dollars from the consumers, have **usurped a taxing power** that solely belongs to government. Included, of course, would be the usurious interest charges of the private banking system and all transactions involving interest-bearing debt resulting in invalid foreclosures.

2. **Judicial determinations.** The constitutional guarantees of the 5th and 14th Amendments, as already mentioned, would provide solid legal grounds for the sovereign people to seek redress in courts of equity and before established committees and commissions.

There are unquestionably, and irrefutably, judicial actions before bars of justice so that a full restitution of assets (the nation's work capability) can be made to the sovereign people.

3. **Eminent Domain.** This inherent power, invested in the sovereign citizenry in the Constitution, could play a major role in directly returning deprived assets to the people. It need not be confiscation since the people could create their own credit, based on the productive potential of a "National Cooperative Commonwealth", and buy outright the technology, pro-

202

ductive machinery and natural resources invalidly owned at the present time

Finally, we should give thought to the fact that the real economic power that the people have a right to is not the tangible property that now exists in factories, buildings, skyscrapers, millions of cars, appliances, warehouses bulging with sundry products, or even the whole infrastructure of the nation.

True wealth is the **knowledge and technological potential to duplicate all the foregoing a thousandfold!**

It would be realistic to say to the monopolies, "Keep your ill-gotten gains but we are determined to employ the nation's **unused productive capability,** exceeding many times current employed capability, in order to provide a decent, wholesome, equitable and non-violent life for every solitary being in this nation."

It is naïve to believe that those currently exercising despotic economic, financial and political power would take the foregoing steps. These steps will be taken when sufficient people are enlightened as to the flawed economic system and vampiristic private banking system that burdens the nation and have deprived the people of their wealth and assets.

34

The Cornerstones of the Commonwealth

BEFORE DEALING with the practical functioning of the Commonwealth we should have a broad picture as to the cornerstones upon which it solidly rests and an appreciation as to the basic human rights it will provide equally for every solitary citizen.

There are three basic pillars providing ballast and support for the whole national structure of the Commonwealth. They may appear as very elementary but in the context of all human relations they are extremely fundamental and important.

Every human being is equally important

Within the Commonwealth there are no favorites. Every person comes into life with equally inherent rights. Quoting from the *Desiderata* "You are a child of the Universe and no less than the trees and the stars you have a right to be here."

And that inherent right underscores your equal claim to the natural abundance of this planet, including the airwaves and all levels of energy, and the right to equal participation in developing optimum character and cosmic awareness.

Every person, irrespective of race, color, religion, gender, nationality or sexual orientation, pleads its claim to equal importance, based not on some decree of charitable government, but on its equal social, economic and political rights. We will cover such rights in our next chapter.

The Quality of Life is Paramount

The worth of government structure and all institutions, must be weighed and evaluated as to how they enhance human beings. Human beings are not meant to serve things. The role of government, all institutions and all structures must serve and improve the quality of life of humans. Only as man-made structures improve the quality of life do they have relevancy

Up the centuries spiritual leaders have appeared with messages embodying the highest reverence for life and subordinating all physical human-created things to the spiritual essences and needs of the people. Tragically, the structures that have been set up to house and proselyte the "inspired word" gradually became more important than the precepts meant to guide the people.

A parallel contradiction has persisted relative to our political idealism. Government institutions, agencies, regulations and their imposing buildings have come to have more importance, and sway, than the inherent rights of every citizen to "life, liberty and the pursuit of happiness" as accentuated in the Declaration of Independence.

Assuredly, the only role of government, institutions and things is to provide a wholesome and equitable environment in which the quality of life is paramount for every man, woman and child in this nation.

Absolute Power of the Sovereign People

The people must have absolute power over their lives and destiny. The most knowledgeable men and women should be elected to government office to research and recommend policy and action. The electorate should render the final decisions. Only complete dispersal of power in the society can preclude the corrupting influence of both economic and political power.

Thomas Jefferson encompassed in one paragraph the foregoing concept of where the ultimate powers of society should be placed. He succinctly stated:

> **I know of no safe depository of the ultimate power of society but the people themselves, and if we think them not enlightened enough to exercise their control with a wholesome discretion, the remedy is not to take it from them but to inform their discretion by education.**

Jefferson clearly foresaw that prostituted power, both political and economic, could arise in the nation and through its dominance misinform, and mislead, the people and then contend that the people were not qualified to exercise their sovereignty. In penning the Declaration of Independence, Jefferson made clear that no usurpation of power should replace the inherent power of the people.

Isn't it significant that the writers of the Constitution didn't state in the Preamble "We the corporate monopolists" or "We the private bankers" or "We the media moguls" but stated *We the People of the United States, in Order to form a more perfect Union, establish Justice, insure domestic Tranquillity, provide for the common defense, promote the general Welfare, and secure the Blessings of Liberty to ourselves and our Posterity, do ordain and establish this Constitution for the United States of America"?*

Clearly, the only safe depository of the ultimate powers of the society are the **sovereign people themselves!**

In the next chapter we will focus on the inviolate human rights of every citizen within the framework of a National Cooperative Commonwealth.

35

Equal human rights

A National Cooperative Commonwealth would mark an end to all forms of discrimination. It would recognize that every member of the society, irrespective of race, color, religion, nationality, gender or sexual orientation had **inviolate and equal human rights.** No longer would there be African-American rights, Native American rights, Hispanic rights, gay-lesbian or women's rights. There would only be **human rights.**

Exercise of equal human rights would no longer be pleaded from a position of economic or political weakness but would arise from every person's ability to command them from having **equal status** and **equal strength** in the Commonwealth.

Human rights would be non-negotiable. No person could be deprived of them. They could only be implemented.

Equal Right to Life Itself

The first priority of the Commonwealth would be to protect and preserve life, particularly in regard to the nation's children. To this end every individual would permanently receive a basic annual dividend in twelve monthly allotments in sufficient amount to supply him or her with the elementary necessities of life. **Poverty** and the **hunger duress** would be removed from the daily existence of every person.

It would compassionately end all forms of welfarism, charity and the dependence on relatives or friends for sustaining life. The stigma of seeking public relief and the whole spectrum of bureaucratic red-tape would have been eliminated.

Equal Right to Health Care

Under the Commonwealth there would come into being a "holistic" health care system that related to body, mind and spirit. All are interdependent and reinforce each other when each is properly nourished. There would be much emphasis on preventive care with special concern for children in terms of nutrition and pre-natal care.

Health care would no longer be dealt with as a product subject to all the current abuses of price gouging, exploitation and fraud in the market place. With social and economic stresses minimized, and a safe, uncontaminated environment, a nation of healthy people would make for an optimum healthy society!

Equal Right to Education

From infancy up to adulthood, and through a lifetime, there would be full and equal opportunity for every person to develop his or her talents to the fullest degree. There is no way that any one, especially the young, can compete in job or social status without having equal educational opportunity. It is an inherent right that the Commonwealth would fulfill and implement for every person.

Self-esteem and ballast in life would come from a constant pursuit of knowledge, increasing one's self-reliance and making one an equal participant in any chosen field of endeavor and an equal participant as a citizen in the functioning of government.

Equal Right to Work

All wealth is some form of taking natural resources, including the airways, and combining them with human skill and human know-how. To deny a person work is denying the person an **inherent right to partnership with Nature itself.**

Natural resources are here as a cosmic legacy, as an endowment of an impartial Creator, and no person, or group of persons, has any rightful power to restrict the availability of those resources from use by the people, including oncoming generations.

Under the Commonwealth every vestige of joblessness would be erased out of the economy. The uniqueness of the Commonwealth is that it could accommodate the fullest employment of the nation's laborsaving technology and at the same time provide for 100% employment.

Equal Right to Voice

Under the Commonwealth every citizen would have a positive and equal voice. All candidates would be nominated by petition and direct primaries would determine the final candidates. All campaigns would be underwritten by **public funding** with equal opportunity for each candidate to present herself or himself.

The power to elect would carry with it the power **to recall** any officeholder who breaks his contract with those who elected him or her. The most vital provision would be **final decisions by the sovereign people** precluding every aspect of political chicanery and abuse of power in all high office.

It would usher in and fulfill the much-touted concept of "Participatory Democracy".

Having set down how the sovereign people can retrieve their rightful ownership and control of the working capacity of this nation, and having set down the cornerstones and basic human rights, we will now commence to present the actual operations of a **National Cooperative Commonwealth.**

~ 36 ~
Functioning of the Commonwealth

WHILE THIS BOOK has been written primarily to focus on the devastating role of private banking, it is necessary to have an economic framework within which an honest and relevant monetary system can operate. The innovative system of banking that will function within the **Commonwealth** adheres to all the basic premises and rightful role of "money" that we have brought out in our coverage of money and credit.

It completely supplants the current iniquitous operations of private banking within the Federal Reserve System.

What a breath of fresh air will waft into the homes of every citizen when it is realized that all the needs of the nation can be automatically funded without any of the burdens of interest-bearing debt or the confiscatory taxes of bureaucratic government!

A question will automatically arise in the minds of many that in our proposing radical economic changes our Representative Republic is politically in jeopardy. Nothing is farther from the truth. We would continue to have a Congress, a Judicial System and a President with his cabinet.

All modifications in political structure would be made with the imperative need of enhancing the democratic process in terms of "government by the authority and rule of the people".

Most emphatically the principle of democracy would hold sway within all the departments and agencies conducting the economic needs of the society. It is uncanny how the sovereign people could democratically coordinate and unleash the full productive capability of the nation efficiently and equitably..

With the total work capability owned and controlled by the sovereign people there would be no limitation to providing an abundant life for all.

Department of Economic Coordination

THIS DEPARTMENT would be the most important department in the democratic functioning of the total economy. It would be the hub of all economic activity. It is within this most vital department that the nation's whole economic **coordination** would take place without any of the restraints and debt-burdens of private banking..

Production and services would be geared solely for use instead of profit. All the people, the total citizenry, would enjoy the good life commensurate with the full utilization of all natural resources, technological know-how and plant machinery.

Would this Department be a politically appointed entity, or agency, such as we have under private capitalism? By no means.! This Department (DEC) would be made up of the elected representatives of every economic endeavor, either in goods or services, that would operate in the nation.

There would be proportionate representation according to the number engaged in each area of endeavor. The peers of each group would exercise their constitutional prerogative of "one person, one vote" and elect their economic representatives the same as they elect their political representatives.

How does the **DEC (Department of Economic Coordination)** function? It functions fundamentally the same way that a renovated Congress will function, with the DEC at all times being responsive to the wishes and directions of all the employees, both skilled and unskilled, including the consumers of the Commonwealth. While the principle operation is the coordinating of the nation's work capability to meet the over-all consuming needs of the entire citizenry, it would be departmentalized for specific duties, which we will consider shortly.

It would be within the scope of this Department that a gradient scale of individual worth would be negotiated determining how each would exercise purchasing power against all goods and services. Most importantly it would be within this department, with national worker representation, that the Commonwealth's total annual needs could be predetermined so that there could be coordinating and budgeting of all work effort.

An uncanny circumstance is that the basic structure of the Commonwealth would be the same as all current corporations. No one could question its Americanism. It would have both Common shares and Preferred shares giving each individual claims against the Commonwealth's total production of goods and services.

A special sustaining feature of the Common Share would be its provision that every person be guaranteed the elementary necessities of life, thus removing throughout his or her lifetime the duress and spectre of hunger.

Of course, it is the Common Share that would give every person a **positive voice** in the conducting of the Commonwealth's business.

Mr. Pelley in his book "No More Hunger," in presenting a "Christian Commonwealth," proposed the division of the Preferred Shares into **Merit** shares and **Realty** shares. The **Merit** shares would represent the wage-dividends a worker received, over and above his subsistence claim, for work he performed in producing either goods or services.

The **Realty** shares would represent the equity or full ownership that each had in a home that is immune from foreclosure or loss of any kind. This unique feature of the Commonwealth will be covered when we deal with the Department of Housing.

We find these divisions of Preferred Shares most adequate and workable in the structuring of the **Commonwealth.**

Let us now focus on the three important supportive agencies of the **DEC** (Department of Economic Coordination):

Agency of Work Capability

This Agency, **AWC**, would have at its fingertips the total producing capacity of the Commonwealth, not only as to the workers in every field but the work-hours, or work-days, needed to produce and make available all goods and services. It would have an updated record of the Commonwealth's total resources, its actual production plants, its total service facilities, and the present and projected research and technology.

There would be the fullest opportunity to bring optimum efficiency to the national workplace. The **AWC** would determine the location of work facilities, the need for relocation of any facility, and the need for additional facilities. It would place strong focus on making each region of the Commonwealth as self-sufficient as possible, eliminating waste in energy and time that is involved in transporting the same kind of goods back and forth across the whole nation.

We have already referred to the **"Hearings on the Impact of Automation on Employment."** The emerging conclusion was that if the nation employed its best technological know-how, only 10 percent of the workforce would be needed to not only produce all of the nation's goods and services but also the 40 percent of all products that are shipped abroad.

This would mean, parenthetically, that in dividing the work effort of the Commonwealth in producing its basic goods and services it would be only necessary for each individual of the nation's roughly 130,000,000 workforce to put in less than one day a week.

The other 90 percent of work effort would be in all areas of public service, and personal pursuits, that focused on the citizen's intellectual, cultural and spiritual betterment. With a lifetime of education and health care guaranteed every person from infancy to death, one can readily envision the scope of services that would be entailed in these two basic areas alone.

The Commonwealth would usher in a human environment that lifted all individuals onto a plateau of performing and living that related to inner sensitivities and the motivation to serve others. All the areas of arts, music, painting and drama would enjoy a resurgence of expression. Not to be excluded would be all the forms of wholesome recreation and the whole spectrum of sports, both public and private.

Before covering the other agencies within the major **Department of Economic Coordination**, the "Agency of Consumer Enlightenment" and the "Agency of Scientific Development," it is timely to consider how the individual worth of one person is determined against that of all others.

37

Determining Individual Worth

THE ANSWER to this question is immediately forth-coming since the process for so doing is basically not unlike that of current labor-management negotiations. The major difference is that workers of the present have to bargain with the corporate owners who have a self-interest in arbitrarily dictating work value and work compensation.

Within the Commonwealth the workers are the cooperative owners of the nation's productive plant so there is a **mutuality** of economic goals.

Throughout history, varying groups of workers, skilled and unskilled, have banded together in guilds, trade unions, associations and professional groups, all vying for what each believed the public would pay for their services. Unfortunately, all efforts of "collective bargaining" up the centuries have been subject to the entrenched abnormal levels of economic and political power.

Consequently, there has not been a level playing field for negotiations and the result has been, as existing at the present, multi-million-dollar salaries and lucrative stock bonuses to the few at the top, under- payment to the majority, and no payment at all to millions of unemployed workers, the outcasts of "down-sizing" and "out-sourcing."

Clearly, determining the worth of individuals is either dictated by authority or it is democratically negotiated.

The first step under the Commonwealth, exactly as happens in the workplace today, would be for the peers of every work endeavor and service, including all areas of government, to determine a gradient scale. In view of technology, the wage-differential would be extremely narrow and the number of divisions of labor would be minimized.

The next step would be for the elected representatives of each work or service endeavor to meet at the Department of Economic Coordination, perhaps with the Agency of Work Capability, and negotiate comparative worth as to skill and risks at each group level. Thus, democratically, a work rating, or **SR** (Skill Rate) could be determined and assigned to every work and service role in the Commonwealth.

The Purchasing power or **Merit dividends** of each individual would simply be his or her **SR** times the **period of work** that was performed.

The total Merit dividends, along with the subsistence income of the total people, would constitute the Commonwealth's GDP (Gross Domestic Product). Any over-all dollar figure could be assigned to the GDP as long as the pro-rated buying power of the total workers, or citizens, totaled the same amount.

The importance of this economic equation is to insure that the people can acquire all goods and services which have been pre-determined and produced as the annual needs of the Commonwealth.

Under the Commonwealth the total work force is all inclusive of every solitary person in every occupation and endeavor. This includes, along with all areas of manufacturing and the whole spectrum of services, those directly extracting raw products from Mother Earth (those involved in farming, mining, lumbering,

219

stock-raising and fishing, to name the principle ones) and all levels of government.

No one is excluded from being both contributor to and beneficiary of the Commonwealth.

Thus, within the national framework of total needs and total citizens, a whole economy can be coordinated and individual worth determined. Each has a **stake** in the national productive capacity. Each has the **full benefit** of advancing technology to provide an abundant society. And each has a **self-interest** in promoting efficiency and maintaining integrity in all operations.

Technology fully and constructively employed will be the great equalizer in determining personal worth and compensation. Even now it is realistic to recognize that the most skilled person's contribution physically and mentally, particularly in productive areas, exceeds only to a small degree that of the menial laborer when sophisticated technology is employed.

It is more than utopian fantasizing to envision a time in the Commonwealth's future when science blended with religion on a high spiritual level would equate all human endeavors on the premise of "give according to your ability and take according to your needs." . . .

38

Two Other Important Agencies

THE Agency of Consumer Enlightenment would replace the entire seductive, wastrel, and multi-billion-dollar annual role of current commercial advertising. It would mark the end of catchpenny, endless sales pitches, billboards desecrating the landscape and the whole area of media devotion to consumer exploitation.

On an average 30.4 percent of airtime of local news consists of commercials. As to the makeup of the actual news itself, crime stories comprise 26.9 percent of the TV news broadcast.

What a change would occur with the **Agency of Consumer Enlightenment!** There would be exclusive focus on the quality of goods and services that were provided by American workers. Constantly, **ACE** would present by print, radio and TV the latest scientific developments pertaining to products and services. There would be a constant updated coverage of designs and styles that evolved out of disciplines in both aesthetics and engineering.

Just as constantly, the consumers would be feeding back their likes and dislikes via electronic communications as to their preferences regarding cars, appliances, clothing, sporting equipment, homes and every product and service making up the Commonwealth's GDP (Gross Domestic Product)

The single goal of the **Agency of Consumer Enlightenment** would be to enlighten and educate the consumers and periodically take surveys to determine democratically their needs and their desires and assuring them a positive voice in the economic functioning of the Commonwealth.

The final agency within the Department of Economic Coordination would be the **Agency of Scientific Development.** The **ASD** would encompasses the whole area of Buckminster Fuller's concept of **design science,** "doing more with less," stressing quality in the producing of all goods and services.

It encompasses the removing of all grueling and stultifying work from the society. And, most importantly, it gives human beings unmandated time to fulfill their creative and cultural urges.

By no means would this Agency be restricted to production and services. It would equally, and more vitally, deal with advancing science and technology in all areas of education, in all the many facets of medicine and health care, and in all the areas of environment and space exploration. No field or endeavor or inquiry would be excluded from scientific scrutiny or evaluation.

The "Union of Concerned Scientists" in their quarterly publication **Earthwise** for Summer 2000 focuses on the fact that "transportation is the single largest source of air pollution and that our cars and trucks emit more carbon dioxide, the primary source of global warming, than most countries emit from all sources combined." They stress the need to adopt Zero Emission Vehicle (ZEV) programs which would pave the way for electric, fuel cell and hybrid vehicles.

Alternative non-polluting sources of energy such as solar and wind would have the full attention of the ASD. The **Natural Business Lobas Journal** stated

222

that 1999 "was a record year for wind power, the fastest growing energy technology of the decade." More than 3,600 megawatts of wind-energy generating capacity was installed in 1999, bringing the total worldwide capacity to about 13,400 MW (megawatts).

To put that in context: One MW can power about 250 average American homes. 3,600 MW is about the capacity of three larger nuclear power plants, and 13,400 is almost enough to power the state of New Jersey. The **Natural Business Lohas Journal** (March/April 2000)

The greatest potential for unlimited clean energy would be the successful harnessing of nuclear fusion. One can be assured that **the Agency for Scientific Development** would have a crash program to achieve this goal. Real steps could be taken when all research and experimenting could be carried on devoid of current monopolistic self-interests.

Today, 80 percent of the nation's scientists are engaged directly or indirectly in working for giant corporations in perfecting weapons of destruction. Or they are employed in engineering built-in obsolescence so that products have a short life span, providing a perpetual cycle of profit taking and do not result in unmovable inventory.

Under the Commonwealth the **ASD** would attract the finest, innovative minds in all scientific disciplines. In their specialized roles, their contributions would .be of the highest order and would command commensurate recognition.

~ 39 ~
End of private banking

THE DEMISE of the Federal Reserve System would abruptly occur with the innovative role of the Commonwealth's **Department of the Treasury.** This Department would be central to the "monetary" functioning of the whole economy. It would signal the death knell for the whole litany of unpayable debts, strangling interest, burdening loans and wholesale foreclosures.

It would mark the liberation of the people from economic inequity and wholesale exploitation. It would be an awakening to a new era of prosperity and economic justice.

We have come full circle in our presentation from the hypothetical island community wherein the Islanders set up an "accountant" to record the "contribution-claims" of each worker to the current role, although more encompassing, of a national **"accounting system of banking."** Positively, the control and function of the nation's economic "blood stream" would be, in the hands of the sovereign people.

In the words of President Lincoln, the Commonwealth would be fulfilling "the supreme prerogative of the government."

Our hypothetical island community presented a number of basic features that are inherent in the functioning of our Commonwealth. Funding for all endeavors, the underwriting of all effort to produce products and services, comes into play automatically as there is work to be done. There is no need to go to private bankers, non-producers, who have the exclusive power of "manufacturing" credit-loans in the form of interest-bearing debt.

Secondly, on the hypothetical island the "contribution-claims," were directly related to the goods and services produced so that in the people's hands was a purchasing power that would buy all that had been produced. We quoted generously from Dr. Soddy's book **Wealth, Virtual Wealth and Debt** to underscore the fact that real wealth had to relate to human effort in the actual production of goods and services.

Remember Soddy stating:

> If we have available energy, we may maintain life and produce every material requisite necessary. That is why the flow of energy should be the primary concern of economics. In a world which has adequate supplies of energy, scientific knowledge and inventions for utilizing it, and the man-power able and willing to perform the necessary duties and services, poverty and destitution are purely artificial institutions. . . .

Two additional paragraphs are most pertinent:

> The variation of the purchasing power of money exposes the community to wholesale injustice on the one side and undeserved gain on the other, as assuredly as if the one set had been despoiled of their belongings by the other by robbery and violence.

> But worse than all, it paves the way to the economic subjugation of humanity to monetary power because of the confusion in the minds of people between money and wealth. By substituting for the "conception of a realized amount" "a

periodical receipt' of an infinitude of future interest payments, it tries to condemn to eternal slavery generations not yet born.

It is also to important to recall President Lincoln's clear distinction between "work" and "capital." Work always has to precede capital. Capital can have no real existence without the presence of work. Lincoln stated:

> They hold that labor is prior to, and independent of capital; that in fact, capital is the fruit of labor, and could never have existed if labor had not first existed; that labor can exist without capital, but that capital could never have existence without labor.
>
> Hence, they hold that labor is the superior, greatly superior of capital.

It is well to reread Thomas Edison's interview in the New York Times which brings out the salient point that a nation should only be limited in what it can do by its resources, its human element, its machines and technology. **Debt-free funding should come into existence automatically for all enterprises**.

It is against the foregoing fundamental thinking of three economic intellects that we can readily grasp the soundness and relevancy of how the National Cooperative Commonwealth could unleash its full work capability without any of the burdens of interest-bearing debt.

Follow now how facilely and practically the **Department of the Treasury,** in conjunction with the **Department of Economic Coordination,** would conduct the economic business of the Commonwealth.

The **Department of the Treasury** would, in conjunction with the regional and branch offices, establish for every citizen in the Commonwealth a credit account to be exercised against the nation's total goods and services. Each credit account would be a combination of the Common share "sustenance" credit plus the Preferred "merit" credit based on the person's contribution to the Commonwealth's GDP (Gross Domestic Product).

The total credit accounts of all persons in the Commonwealth, as we have stressed many times, would be equal to the total cost of all goods and services that are available for purchase. We say "available for purchase" since in an abundant society with the potential to employ the most advanced technology, many basic products and services would be without cost to every citizen.

At the end of the year all unused credit would be canceled and at the beginning of the next year a new annual credit would be placed to the account of every member of the Commonwealth. Assuredly, by now everyone grasps that the total credit of the **Department of the Treasury** established annually upon its books is not something that is borrowed into existence.

The total credit is simply **monetizing or measuring the total production of the Commonwealth in both goods and services and setting up individual credit accounts to be exercised against the established national credit.**

An "accounting system of banking" would not only mean an end to all the encumbrances and inequities of interest, liens, mortgages and foreclosures but it would also mean an end to the whole bureaucratic spectrum of confiscatory taxation which extorts a third of the taxpayer's earnings each year.

Every cost of government, or of the Commonwealth, whether in the cost of raw stock or refined goods, or in the wages of the most menial laborer or the highest executive, would be all inclusive in the Commonwealth's annually determined **National Operating Credit.**

The question arises: Who determines that all-inclusive Credit? The people through their elected representatives, who are constantly monitoring all the Commonwealth's Departments, would determine it democratically. They would in turn recommend to the total members, or citizens, the Commonwealth's needs including humanitarian assistance to people in distressed lands.

After the electorate's final acceptance of the recommendations, all implementation would be set in motion.

Inviolate Individual ID and Debit Card

The most important document every citizen would possess would be his or her ID (identification) card imprinted with his or her personal identification. The individual's picture and fingerprints would make the card inviolate to the individual and it would be of no employable value to anyone who stole it. With every person having his or her own ID card, there would be no incentive to steal someone else's card.

A cashless society would become a reality, marking an end to robbery of all kinds. And too often, subsequent murder.

A citizen's verified ID would give him or her a **debit card** that could purchase all products and services and the transactions would electronically debit his or her credit account at a Regional Bank. Debit cards are currently used to buy gas and groceries, pay utility bills and make countless other payments.

The major, and critical, difference between the debit card of the Commonwealth and current credit cards (Visa, Master, Discover, American Express, etc.) is that the former is premised on the individual's annual stake in the nation's total productive capability and is devoid of the cancerous role of interest-bearing indebtedness.

Nationalizing Foreign Assets

A significant role for the **Department of the Treasury** would be in the process of "nationalizing" foreign corporations and assets. In the past, in times of war or purported threats to our national security, our government has frozen foreign assets, both liquid and tangible, with adjustments made at a later time.

We have already noted that American multi-national corporations have at the present time similar hundreds of billions of dollars in foreign holdings as their foreign corporate counterparts have holdings in this country. Thus, there could be equalizing steps taken with credit balances determined.

We must face the stark reality that the foreign investments by the multi-national corporations of the United States along with the corporate conglomerates of other countries has had the primary goal of exploiting the work and resources of each other's land. Giant grain companies, oil cartels, auto and chemical manufacturers, electronic companies, and particularly banking and investment entities, are in the predatory business of making hundreds of billions of dollars in profit for their limited stockholders.

A most serious development of recent years is our nation becoming beholden to the accumulative U. S. debt held by other countries. The most threatening nation is China holding a half trillion dollars in American securities. This resulted by China using her gain in the trade deficit, 400 billions annually, and exchanging her sale of shoddy goods to us for our prime government securities.

Assistance to citizens in other countries is an exploitive game played on a global scale. Belatedly, it is recognized more and more that unconscionable **globalization,** especially as practiced against undeveloped countries, is a basic cause of worldwide terrorism. Hypocritically, those entrenched in economic power are against terrorism unless "they" are the terrorists.

Mark this well: The integrity, vitality and potency of the National Cooperative Commonwealth that we are proposing are dependent on the people's **absolute ownership** and **coordination** of its resources, technology and tools of production.

The Commonwealth's well being, peace and security, and for the generations yet unborn, cannot be dependent of or beholden to the dictates of foreign speculative interests.

The Commonwealth's **Department of the Treasury** would mean liberation from every vestige of interest-bearing debt and would truly function as the economic "blood stream" of the Commonwealth! . . .

40

Department of Housing

WE HAVE COVERED to this point the basic economic features of the Commonwealth. We have explained how each member exercises purchasing power by way of a claim to basic survival by virtue of his or her Common Share and we have explained how each member exercises his or her further purchasing power by way of the Preferred "merit" Share.

Most significantly, we have shown that the total buying power of the total citizenry would buy the Commonwealth's total annual goods and services. Each year the **Department of the Treasury** would set up a new account for every person.

Next to having constant employment and a guaranteed income there is nothing as important to each family as being secure in their own home free from taxation and foreclosure. For this reason we will cover with some detail home ownership within the framework of the Commonwealth.

The **Department of Housing** would have the full responsibility of registering and facilitating the buying and selling of all homes in the Commonwealth. It would be the guarantor that every home was safe from any threat of foreclosure since any and all payments would be toward actual ownership.

What a giant step forward in the ease and speed of selling and buying homes with the innovation of the other Preferred Share called **"Realty"** or simply "R" shares! This stock feature, along with both the

Common and Preferred "merit" Shares must be fully accredited to Mr. Pelley in his outlining of a "Christian Commonwealth" in his book **No More Hunger.**

From the earliest frontier days up to the half of the Twentieth Century the majority of families have occupied a house for the larger part of their lifetime. Generally, homes were handed down from one generation to the next. Increasingly, the nation's homeowners have evolved into a transient population with families staying in one locality for only a matter of a few years or in many cases a shorter time.

The problem entailed in change of location has been a constant hassle, and hurdle, of first seeking a buyer and then in turn purchasing a home elsewhere. Months of anxiety and impatience are endured with high pressure Realtors urging bargain sales with the mover's interest secondary to the agent's commissions.

What exhilaration the homeowner would feel at the ease in which changing homes and location. could take place! The **Department of Housing** would expedite change and location with dispatch and without any profiteering expenses. Here is how it would work.

First, he or she would appear at the Department's Realty Board within their county and receive a number of "Realty Shares" equal to the appraised value of the home. Their home would then be listed unoccupied and available for a new owner at a specified time.

With the seller in possession of "R" shares, he or she would simply avail themselves of the computerized listings in the Realty Board Office and could determine what desired type of home was available in a location of their liking. Technology is at present employed in many Realtor's offices that allows potential buyers to view, via the computer, both the outside and inside of homes at unlimited distances.

When a desired, unoccupied home is located, the new buyer now turns his or her "R" shares over to the Commonwealth Realty Board in the new location toward purchase of the new home. If one doesn't have sufficient "R" shares to cover the listed value of the new home, then the difference can be made up by monthly payments from one's Merit Share earnings.

If one's amount of "R" shares exceeds the appraised value of the new home, the extra shares would be recorded and be available later for the acquiring of a home of a higher value.

The Commonwealth would stipulate that it was the home, and not the land, that represented ownership, and that the owner had to occupy the home a minimum of time, perhaps eight months a year, in order to preclude homes being denied someone else.

Temporary exchanging of homes by families in different locations would be quite acceptable. Also, there would be other ample facilities for all those wishing to enjoy seasonal recreations or relief from extreme cold or hot weather.

This would be especially true, also, where there were scenic areas of lakes and mountains.

Custodial Care

With the Commonwealth desirous of making home-life as relaxing and unencumbered as possible, it would provide all upkeep and maintenance such as plumbing, electrical, painting and landscaping. On the other hand, it would encourage owners to add their own personal touches to both the inside and the outside of their homes.

The Commonwealth's custodial care would be no different than the kind of spontaneous care apartment dwellers receive at well-managed housing complexes. Even more relevant and pertaining to the Commonwealth's housing are the Co-op Apartments in which there is "ownership" along with custodial care.

Cooperative Apartments, especially with their eating accommodations, and varied shops, are positive and relevant forerunners to the National Cooperative Commonwealth.

A Home as One's "Castle"

Home ownership within the Commonwealth would be inviolate and no longer would families live under the threat of foreclosure. Lending institutions and their vampiristic interest charges, along with the confiscatory taxing of bureaucratic government, would all be relics of an archaic past. All transactions of buying and selling homes could be freely made in a matter of hours devoid of all pressures.

The most tragic circumstance is, of course, with the homeless. No nation can call itself civilized that forces hundred of thousands of its citizens, many disabled, half of them women and children, to find protection from the elements in cardboard boxes, under bridges, in alleys or the confines of their cars.

The existing intolerable condition of the homeless is criminal when they are denied sufficient wages to buy a home, and when the nation has the capability to build to surfeit all necessary homes.

The **Department of Housing** would continuously monitor the housing needs of the Commonwealth. There would be no waiting list for anyone, particularly the young seeking homes for the first time. Across the length and width of America it would be the end to homelessness.

In security and human uplift every home in the Commonwealth would truly be the owner's "castle"!

41

Peace with Economic Justice

THERE ARE other important departments but our concern was to cover those departments directly related to the functioning and economic vitality of the Commonwealth. We wanted to establish the two most vital economic needs of each person in the Commonwealth. This was having permanent income and a secure home. With permanent shelter, and assured purchasing power for all other basic necessities, like clothing and food, including recreation and travel, all could enjoy a happy prosperous life within an abundant society.

This is all realistically possible with the adoption of a **National Cooperative Commonwealth** within which would function an honest monetary system. Inherent in our overall proposals was the goal to achieve economic justice for the total citizenry.

The most challenging barrier to an equitable and peaceful society is the economic burden of the privately owned and operating Federal Reserve System. Therefore my main focus throughout my book has been to indict, with a scathing "bill of particulars," the central, ruinous role of interest-bearing debt.

The two most important goals of society, or for that matter the goals of the world, are **economic justice** and **universal peace**. Both are interdependent on each other. Neither has any reality without dual realization of both. It is unrealistic to think of any real peace in our society when millions of children cry for food and families are unable to pay their bills and mentally break under unbearable economic stresses.

And, of course, the economic ills and dire hardships of our nation fade into insignificance in light of the literally billions in the world who haven't adequate food, sufficient clean water, health facilities, schools and the basic necessities to protect and preserve life.

Individuals and nations responsible for this human tragedy on a world scale stand irrefutably indicted when the natural resources and developed work capability are present to meet abundantly the needs of all the people.

A Blackened Cinder Tumbling through Space

Even if economic well being and economic justice were achieved, what meaning would such goals be if our nation, or any other nation, purposely or accidentally launched the horrendous nuclear weaponry that exists and the world became an uninhabitable blackened cinder tumbling through space? The question calls for somber and critical reflection!

In an opening address, April 24, 2000, to a U. N. conference on the 1968 Nuclear Nonproliferation Treaty, Secretary-general Kofi Annan called the threat of nuclear war a "terrifying possibility." He warned "Nuclear conflict remains a very real, and very terrifying possibility at the beginning of the 21st Century. This is the stark reality confronting you today."

Annan also warned that another cornerstone of arms control, the 1972 Anti-Ballistic Missile (ABM) Treaty, was being derailed by pressure to allow the creation of a limited missile defense system. He forewarned, "This pressure, to deploy national missile defenses, is jeopardizing the ABM Treaty and could well lead to a new arms race."

In today's unsettled world of terrorism and prevalent weapons of mass destruction, and our young men and women dying each day in the undeclared war in Iraq. it behooves us most seriously to get an honest perception as to our role in the world.

There has to be courageous appraisal of the forces and influences that promote, and profit, from bloody carnage.

The Phantom Devil

In-depth analysis of both "hot" and "cold" wars inevitably leads to the conclusion that it is always economic and political self-interest that engenders hate and mistrust and ulterior purposes to the people of different lands. Charles A. Beard, one of the nation's most astute historians, in his book **The Devil Theory of War** gives a graphic picture of how an unsuspecting people are manipulated into wars.

Persistently and subtly, the people are subjected to carefully patterned propaganda instilling in the minds of the people that a "devil" rules some particular country and it must be destroyed in the interest of "national and world security." Ultimately armed conflict is assured by the multi-national corporate entities swaying the nation politically. The young die while exorbitant profits go to the instigators of war.

There is a critical and pointed lesson to be learned from all the wars and interventions that this nation has been engaged in during the Twentieth Century up to the current quagmire in Iraq. Underscored. should be this indisputable fact: A nation's **foreign policy** is not one **whit greater in integrity and honesty** than the integrity and honesty of its **national policy.**

A national political leadership, and its implemented policies, that denies human rights and is insensitive to human needs at home is going to reflect that same neglect in its policies and actions abroad. That is why, unfortunately, we are so hypocritical and hated by people in so many foreign lands.

~ 42 ~
Collaboration with Tyrants

Under the subterfuge of "democracy" and protecting United States "national security" our marines have periodically during the Twentieth Century interceded in behalf of murderous and despotic regimes. Our brutal policy has taken place throughout the past century going back to the time of the Spanish conquistadors.

In an article appearing in **Common Sense** in 1933 we have the testimony and assessment of our foreign policy during the early part of the past century. General Smedley D. Butler minced no words in characterizing his personal role:

> There isn't a trick in the racketeering bag that the military gang is blind to. It has its "finger men" (to point out enemies), its "muscle men" (to destroy enemies), its "brain guys" (to plan war preparations), and a Big Boss (supernationalistic capitalism).
>
> It may seem odd for me, a military man to adopt such a comparison. Truthfulness compels me to do so. I spent 33 years and 4 months in active military service as a member of our country's most agile military forces, the Marine Corps. I served in all commissioned ranks from a second lieutenant to Major General. And during that period I spent most of my time being a high-class muscle man for Big Business, for Wall Street and for the bankers. In short, I was a racketeer, a gangster for capitalism.

I suspected I was just a part of a racket at the time. Now I am sure of it. Like all members of the military profession, I never had an original thought until I left the service. My mental facilities remained in suspended animation while I obeyed the orders of the higher-ups. This is typical with everyone in the military service.

Thus I helped make Mexico and especially Tampico safe for American oil interests in 1914. I helped make Haiti and Cuba a decent place for National City Bank boys to collect revenues in. I helped in the raping of half a dozen Central American republics for the benefit of Wall Street. The record of racketeering is long. I helped purify Nicaragua for the international banking house of Brown Brothers in 1909-12. I brought light to the Dominican Republic for American sugar interests in 1916. In China in 1927 I helped to see to it that the Standard Oil went its way unmolested.

During those years, I had, as the boys in the back room would say, a swell racket. I was rewarded with honors, medals and promotion. Looking back on it, I feel that I might have been given Al Capone a few hints. The best he could do was operate his racket in three city districts. I operated on three continents.

General Butler's assessment of the United States military role in the early part of the Twentieth Century is but prelude to the balance of the 1900s. His role "for Big Business, for Wall Street, for bankers and for capitalism" has been the role of the military up to the present time. Only the killing potential of modern weaponry has been so much more lethal and civilians are the larger number of victims in modern war.

For the larger part of the past century, in our hemisphere, we are witness to the tragic circumstance of our nation collaborating with the brutal regimes of the Batistas, the Trujillos, the Duvaliers, the Pinochets, the Samosas, all oppressors and murderers of innocent citizens in their respective countries.

When Fidel Castro in 1959 led a successful revolution against the Batista government, he was hailed as a liberating leader. However, the moment that he nationalized the giant multi-national corporations in the interest of his people's survival, he was castigated as a tyrant, and an embargo was instituted denying, among other things, needed medicines to Cuban children. Persistent United States policy has focused on the overthrow of Castro.

What is the real fear of succeeding Administrations and the corporate giants entrenched in our nation? It is the fear that other nations in Central and South America would seek to emulate Cuba's liberation, which has installed domestic policies of economic reform including universal health and universal education.

Thus, an unrelenting effort is pursued to bring about regime change under the guise that Castro (now succeeded by his brother, Rowal), is a threat to the security of the United States.

This explains our clandestine support of terrorist groups in Florida that they might assist in derailing the leaders of the Cuban government. A collateral gain, of course, is to capture the Latino vote politically.

It was my personal experience to join a professional fact-finding group that travelled to El Salvador in 1986 to document the struggles of a people who were engaged in a civil war seeking political liberation and surcease from endemic poverty, widespread illiteracy and disease.

We interviewed the life-and-death struggle of those in labor groups, farmer's co-ops, universities, women's groups (like the Co-madres) and non-governmental peace and justice organizations that supported the revolutionary leadership of the FMLN.

As a nation we financed the despotic government of El Salvador, made up of the military and a landed aristocracy of 12 families that owned almost all of the productive land. During the 1980's we poured in four billion dollars to support successive oppressive regimes, trained their "death squads" at the "School of America" at Fort Benning, Georgia, and deceptively claimed it was all done in the name of "national security".

Anyone under the slightest suspicion of not acquiescing to oppressive government was mercilessly tortured. The "death squads" assassinated Eighty thousand **(80,000)** civilians. Sadly, as a nation, we aided and abetted such wholesale destruction of innocent life.

Our group shared the position of our ambassador to El Salvador, Robert White, who stated publicly, "We are on the wrong side!" Summarily, he was removed from his post.

There has been a consistent pattern of collaborating with oppressive governments or employing the marines and the CIA to bring about regime change throughout Central and South American nations. General Butler's indictment, which we printed earlier, covers the scope of our intrigue and military force.

Much earlier the clandestine role of the CIA caused the illegal removal of the people's duly elected President Mossedegh of Iran and replaced him with the U. S. sanctioned Shaw who was brutally indifferent to the needs of the people. And what heinous "crime" had Mossedegh committed? He moved to nationalize the oil wells of Iran for the benefit of the Iranian people.

And what about the duly-elected President of Chile, Salvador Allende, who was forced out of office by the secret operations of the CIA? What were his crimes? He was guilty of installing economic reforms unfavorable to the corporate interests of the United States. Riots were fomented that led to the assassination of Allende and the rise to power of the military tyrant Pinochet.

Another case is our current underwriting of the oppressive government in Columbia to destroy the insurgents (FARCO) striving for economic justice.

And, there are the continuous efforts to overthrow President Hugo Chavez of Venezuela. The hostility of Administrations toward him is readily understood. Chavez has publicly denounced U. S. unilateralism and as the fifth largest exporter of oil in the world does not kowtow to OPEC or the monopolistic oil corporations in the United States.

Rather, he used oil for underwriting needed social programs. As a consequence, the people have given Chavez sustaining support in staving off outside efforts to overthrow him and at the same time have given him consistent political approval.

A most recent case is the kidnapping of duly elected President Jean-Bertrand Aristide of Haiti, transporting him to Africa, and then setting up a military regime favorable to the economic interest of the multinationals in the United States.

And finally, there is the ongoing oppressive and illegal 41-year Israel occupation of Palestine. No U. S. action in the world is as untenable and unjustifiable as that of our Israeli-Palestinian biased position.

While we tenaciously adhere to the United Nation resolutions pertaining to Iraq, we are blind to the UN resolutions 242 and 338 which call for Israel to remove itself from all occupied territories gained by the 1967 war. The U. S. position is in flagrant violation of a people's "right of self-determination" and the provisions of the U. N. Charter.

The needless killing in the Middle East sickens fair-minded people. Except for a few instances, the picture we get via the monopolized media is distorted. The Palestinians are portrayed as the villains when they have for forty-one years struggled to be free of Israeli's illegal occupation of their homeland.

On October 21, 2000 the United Nations in an emergency session approved 96 to 6 a resolution critical of Israeli's brutal role in the Middle East. It cited the bulldozing of homes, the uprooting of olive groves, and indiscriminate missile attacks that killed so many innocent women and children.

The resolution "condemned acts of violence, especially excessive use of force by the Israeli forces against Palestinian civilians." United States and Israel voted against the resolution, and 46 countries abstained.

There is little question that American policy is shaped and maintained by the political influence of the

"American-Israeli Political Action Committee" which reflects the policies of the leading Jewish organizations in the nation.

The Israel Lobby and U. S. Foreign Policy by John J. Mersheimer, Department of Political Science, University of Chicago and Stephen M. Walt, John F. Kennedy School of Government, Harvard University, (March, 2006) is the most definitive and comprehensive Report to be made public as to how U.S. Foreign Policy and U.S. National Security are shaped by the "American-Israel Political Action Committee".

I have only sketchily highlighted some of the U. S. efforts to bring about regime change and increase U. S. global dominance. There has been a consistent pattern that has characterized our interventions and clandestine CIA actions throughout the world

Comprehensive coverage can be found in recent books like **Confessions of an Economic Hit Man** (2004) by John Perkins, **Hegemony or Survival: America's Quest for Global Dominance** (2003) by Noam Chomsky and **Imperial Overstretch** (2004) by Jim Tarbell. and Roger Burbach

It is estimated that U. S. commercial banks along with the World Bank and International Monetary Fund have saddled unsuspecting smaller countries with over **2.3 trillion dollars** in debt by inducing them to accept the underwriting of projects which are non-productive. Burdened with interest they cannot pay, they are easy prey to exploitation and confiscation of their resources.

Author John Perkins presents in his book the deceit and intrigue that has been employed in Ecuador. Panama, Indonesia and other small countries with the goal to get control of their natural resources.. The whole spectrum of deceit, collaboration with oppressive regimes and too often assassination, has been the trademarks of the brutal operations.

A philosophy of "might makes right!" has emerged. We blindly accept the arrogant thinking that the **ability** to exploit the work and resources of other nations, and make regime change, carries with it the **moral right** to do so!

It is reckless and irrational logic. It is violation of International Law and the right to self-determination by all nations however small and however different in political character.

It is a callous indifference to the tens of thousands, tens of millions, who are needlessly made to suffer or to lose their lives. Humans, both military and civilian, become expendable when economic greed and political power are abusively and blindly sought.

We now want to focus on the major wars, the latter half of the Twentieth Century, in which the underlying U.S. goals have been **regime change** and **imperialism.** It is in major conflicts that the magnitude of cost in treasure and lives, both military and civilian, is so stunning and chilling.

We primarily want to deal in some length with World War II, the "mother of all destruction", because morally and ethically it cries for clarity and understanding as to the causes and entities that made it happen.

World War II

THE MOST COSTLY war in lives and treasure was World War II in which fifty three million **(53,000,000)** lives were lost by all the countries involved in the wholesale bloody carnage. We recruited, or drafted, sixteen million young men, and women, who participated in that war. Four hundred and six thousand **(406,000)** gave their lives and tens of thousands came home physically impaired, many as amputees, and others with deeply troubled minds.

No war before, or after, has claimed such colossal sacrifice in lives and treasure. It chills both mind and soul to attempt to envision and grasp what circumstance or motivation could have caused such bloody catastrophe!

Today, most Americans, in fact the vast majority, have been brainwashed to believe that it was a "good war" and the loss of such magnitude of lives and treasure was justified. Our younger generation is unaware of the fact that we were a nation in which the vast number of Americans was opposed to our embroilment in that war.

They are unaware that outstanding members of both Houses of Congress and organizations like "America First" for which Charles A Lindbergh, the "Lone Eagle," was a spokesman, opposed every step that the nation was taking that they knew would lead to inevitable massive deaths on a foreign shore. .

Poll after poll bore out that the vast number of citizens did not want their loved ones again sacrificed in another world war. World War I was too agonizingly vivid in their consciousness. And, they felt comforted in the repeated promise of President Roosevelt that "no American boys will be sent to die on foreign soil"!

An example of the many speeches that President Roosevelt made leading up to our entrance into WWII was on October 26, 1939. In an address to the New York Herald-Tribune Forum, he stated the following:

> **In and out of Congress, we have orators and commentators and others, beating their breasts and proclaiming against sending the boys of American mothers to fight on the battlefields of Europe. That, I do not hesitate to label as one of the worst fakes in current history. It is a deliberate setting up of an imaginary bogeyman.**

> **The simple truth is, that no person in any responsible place in the national administration in Washington, or in any State government, or in any county government, has ever suggested in any shape, manner or form the remotest possibility of sending boys of American mothers to fight on the battlefields of Europe. That is why I label that argument a shameless and dishonest fake.**

A "shameless and dishonest fake"! History, of course, has recorded Roosevelt's statement as deceitful and brazen in light of what happened two short years later.

Charles A. Beard, along with his wife, Mary, are ranked as two of the nation's most outstanding historians.. They have written many books including American **Foreign Policy In the Making 1932-1940, Economic Interpretation of the Constitution** and the **Devil Theory of War,** which we referred to earlier.

The full documentation of the deceptive steps leading to World War II can be found in Beard's book **President Roosevelt and The Coming of the War 1941.** From the time of the passage of the "Neutrality Act" to the enactment of "Lend Lease", to our provocative steps against Japan, Beard chronologically documents U. S. policies and actions that made our entrance into World War II a foregone happening..

The documentation leaves no doubt that the Roosevelt Administration was hell-bent on getting this nation into war with the Axis Powers. There were reasons far deeper and sinister than anything having to do with the nation's security or self-interest. Certainly, there was no threat of "eminent danger" from military forces on the other side of massive oceans that made our embroilment an urgent necessity.

The horrendous reality of World War II was but a prelude to the deceit and lies that would be part of subsequent wars, like Korea, Vietnam and Iraq, with tens of thousands of our nation's finest needlessly dying in faraway lands?

It inexorably led to a national policy of "unilateral, preemptive strike" irrespective of International Law and the wishes of the sovereign people. It was all part of a persistent and reckless policy of **"regime change"** that held sway during the first part of the Twentieth Century and crystallized more firmly leading up to the beginning of the Twenty First?

At some time in the future, historical revisionists will come forth with definitive and undisputed answers to those questions. The historical picture will be all-inclusive as to U. S. action on our continent, that we have briefly covered, but also covering all the wars on other continents.

It was my good fortune to have a personal friend, General Hugh B. Hester, who was a regular contributor to the **Eagle's Eye,** a monthly magazine of which I was the editor. He was a close confidante and I had the good fortune of many visits with him. He served for 34 years with the U. S. Army, was the recipient of the Distinguished Service Medal and the French Legion of Honor, and was present in Germany during the war.

He gave me personal and up-close perspective of World War II, particularly the deceit and hidden motivations for our participation in it.

The rise of Adolph Hitler, and his becoming Chancellor by appointment of President Von Hindenburg, cannot be understood without the background of the Versailles Treaty and the intolerable economic restraints that were placed on the German people at the end of World War One. The "mark" was devalued by manipulations of the dominant German banks, including our Federal Reserve System, so that the life savings of German citizens would barely buy a loaf of bread.

Women were forced into prostitution, children cried for food and abject poverty permeated the land. The nation was desperately crying for change.

If it hadn't been Hitler it would have been some other individual around whom the people would have rallied seeking economic stability and a rightful place amongst nations.

Whatever criticism one can make of German National Socialism (Nazism) one thing is certain. At its core it was an effort to rescue a people from imposed oppression and restore dignity to a conquered land. At the same time it did provide a bold challenge to those nations that feared its rise to power.

Clearly, the world's most powerful nations, England and the United States, did not economically or financially want a revitalized Germany that would be a major contender on the world stage.

Germany had already instituted programs that challenged the exclusive world corporate and banking powers. Intolerable to the central banking systems of England and the United States, and major trans-national corporate entities, was Hitler's introduction of the "Barter System" in which unrefined raw stock of non-industrial nations could be exchanged for finished products by industrial countries like Germany.

Such transactions between nations bypassed the "Bank of International Settlements," an adjunct of the world's central banking systems, and was a major innovation that challenged the economic domination which England and the United States enjoyed.

Ways must be found, however deceptive, that would get Germany engaged in a war that the Allies felt they could win. The dispute between Poland and Germany over the Polish Corridor provided the opportunity.

Uncovering the plot was Tyler Kent, who was a career diplomat and a member of the American Embassy in England. He was alarmed to learn that messages he secretly decoded between Roosevelt and Churchill revealed that they were plotting war with Germany.

They were clandestinely pressuring Poland to adamantly refuse to negotiate with Hitler despite the fact that the Polish Corridor was a legitimate question of mutual concern between both nations.

I got the story directly from Mr. Kent when legal counsel for my father-in-law, William Dudley Pelley, made an appointment for me to solicit Kent's testimony confirming the accuracy of statements that Mr. Pelley was charged with as being false during his "sedition" trial in Washington.

He told me that he was more then willing to testify but needed the protection of being subpoenaed because the State Department had warned him, after his release, that he would be violating the law if he revealed anything learned during his government employment.

Kent felt the strong need to reach prominent members of the U. S. Congress who were opposed to American involvement in WWII. He wanted to apprise them of the secret plotting that was taking place that would embroil the United States. Unfortunately, in his attempt to make contact with them his efforts came to naught when his undercover findings were discovered.

Under Briton's "Defense of the Realm Act" Kent, an American citizen, was arrested without charge and without hearing and given an indefinite sentence to prison. All his constitutional rights were ignored and the United States Administration refused to intercede in his behalf.

Poland succumbed to the pressure of the United States and England and stubbornly refused to negotiate with Germany. An Ultimatum was issued by Hitler, ignored by Poland, and WWII became the sought for reality of Churchill and Roosevelt.

While the military history of the war has been well covered publicly, it is the political maneuvering, chicanery and lying to the American people that one finds in a documented book like Beard's **"President Roosevelt and the Coming of the War 1941"**.

Another book just published the latter part of 2008 is most telling in underscoring the fact that WWII didn't just happen. The book is titled **Churchill, Hitler and the Unnecessary War** by Patrick J. Buchanan. It is well documented and underscores the role of Churchill and Roosevelt in bringing about the war.

World War II didn't just happen. It had a calculated and hidden purpose despite its being labeled as "the best of wars." What a hollow ring to contend that the sacrifice of millions, tens of millions, of the world's population was to "preserve democracy."!

The loss of 53,000,000 million lives! It is mind chilling and soul wrenching to even think of such loss of life and wanton destruction of property? There is no need to call to mind the nightmarish horrors of Nagasaki and Hiroshima where in a matter of seconds nearly 200,000 Japanese were incinerated with thousands on the outskirts dying from radioactive burns.

Or reminding ourselves of the 24-hour firebombing by B-52's of Dresden, a non-military city, leaving upwards of a 100,000 dead.

A barbaric military strategy was introduced toward the end of the war. General Dwight Eisenhower, Supreme Commander of Allied Forces, was charged to carry out deliberate "civilian bombing" in order to **destroy civilian morale of the "enemy"**.

Literally millions of civilians were buried in the rubble of destroyed German and Japanese cities.

Charles Beard in his book chronicles the futile approaches of Japanese envoys to communicate with U. S. leaders for a negotiated peace. Tokyo had been reduced to rubble by American relentless bombing, and the hellish atomic bombs had not as yet been released on Nagasaki and Hiroshima. There was a real opportunity to preclude the world conflagration, which ensued with such horrendous cost in lives.

WWII didn't randomly happen. Nor did it occur to protect U. S. soil. It was **made to happen**. It was contrived by premeditated choice. And the world experienced the unconscionable tragedy. The documentation presented in Beard's and Buchanan's books identifies the perpetrators responsible for the premeditated killing.

For historical accuracy, Churchill and Roosevelt, along with all others who collaborated with them, should be indicted and brought before a court of justice, however belatedly.

WWII was not a just war! Such bloody carnage met none of the historical criteria of a "just" war. First, there was no **imminent danger** to our nation. We were not threatened by the attack of an enemy. Secondly, there must be **informed consent** by the people who underwrite war with their lives and taxes. The people, including the Congress, overwhelmingly, were against our involvement.

And thirdly, the principle of **proportionality** was flagrantly not met in light of the astronomical costs in lives and property against purported results.

Truth is the first casualty of war! Human lives on both sides become cheap and dispensable. Both civilians and warriors are diminished to mere statistics. Sadly, only the losers are charged with atrocities. And an impartial God is shamefully aligned on the side of those with the most devastating weaponry. So it was with our involvement and conduct of WWII.

So it is with all wars!

During contrived wars not only is there the needless death of soldiers and civilians but also there is an onslaught on constitutional rights causing illegal imprisonment and internment. There are countless cases of such victims. I want to single out two cases of grave injustice during WWII.

One was racist in which American citizens of Japanese descent were uprooted from their homes in California and interned in another state for the duration of the war.

Over 120,000 American citizens of Japanese descent were forcefully taken from their homes on the West Coast and transported to quickly constructed internment camps in Nevada. There were no warrants for their arrest, no charges were filed against them, none were allowed to have attorneys for their defense, and all were held incommunicado.

The forced exodus of American citizens, without any protection of their constitutional rights, constitutes a shameful page in United States history. It was prelude to what was to happen to the detainees of the Iraq war.

The second most egregious injustice during WWII was the illegal imprisonment of an American researcher, writer and activist for peace whose only "crime" was exposing flagrant economic injustice in our nation and challenging the illegal acts of the Roosevelt Administration that were inexorably embroiling this nation in an unnecessary war.

This is the case of my father-in-law, William Dudley Pelley, whose illegal conviction Jeffrey Stone has singled out in his book **Perilous Times (2005)** as the most outstanding example of judicial injustice during WWII. His case demands fullest scrutiny because it embodies the whole spectrum of wantonly destroyed constitutional rights that could befall any citizen.

Adelaide, my lifelong partner of sixty-two years, and I devoted considerable chronological coverage of what happened to her Dad in a book called **The Price of Truth** (2008) published by **Trafford Publishers,** Victoria, BC, Canada. We were eager to cover the legal wrongs imposed on him and dispel the distortions that surrounded his life.

~ 44 ~
Continuous Wars!

SINCE WORLD WAR II, in much lesser scope, but just as needless, our nation has pursued untenable foreign policies costing much treasure in lives and destruction. The Congress has embroiled the nation in bloody conflicts without a Constitutional declaration of war. It was as if those in political power had some "divine" right to mass slaughter devoid of any threat to the United States.

In the early 1950s we sent tens of thousands of troops to North Korea purported to stem a communist threat against South Korea. Some 40,000 of our soldiers gave their lives, tens of thousands seriously wounded, fighting not under a Constitutional declaration of war but under the auspices of the United Nation.

Within a decade, during the 1960s, again without a declaration of war, a half million (500,000) Americans were sent to Vietnam with an untenable attempt to replace the 70-year imperialism of the French. The hillsides were decimated by relentless bombing and blood flowed freely in the rice paddies.

Over 60,000 Americans gave their lives and over 200,000 came home blinded, without limbs or seriously troubled in mind and spirit.

In war we don't focus on the deaths and casualties inflicted on our "enemies". It were as if those lost in battle had no fathers, mothers, wives, brothers and sisters to grieve over their absence. It is estimated that over 2,000,000 Vietnamese were killed during the war.

Then the Persian Gulf War in 1990. Under the guise of returning an unelected emir and his royal family to undemocratic power, a quarter million (250,000) troops were transported to the region. Using the latest technology of "smart bombs," "guided missiles" and heavy armored tanks the Iraqi forces were devastated within days.

Enemy soldiers hidden in their trenches were bulldozed over and it is estimated that the majority of the enemy were buried alive.

What was the hidden objective of such carnage? Indisputably, it was to achieve domination of the world oil market in the interest of U. S. trans-national corporate entities.

And now Iraq!

Clearly it is an extension of the Persian Gulf War in seeking absolute domination of the rich oil fields of that area. Clearly, our invasion of Iraq was based on the false premise that she had "weapons of mass destruction," that she had working ties with the Al Qaeda, that she had a nuclear program and was an "imminent threat" to the United States.

All such reasons for war have been exclusively and irrefutably been found wanting and are now recognized as promoted blatant lies.

The deceit and deception that was perpetrated on the Congress and the American people has been documented in a number of books and brought out in testimony before House and Senate Intelligence Committees, including a special 911 Commission bringing to light gross negligence on the part of the Administration in preventing the 911 attacks.

The unauthorized military invasion of Iraq in March 2003 created a bloody prolonged occupation with each month since that time witnessing an increasing number of American soldiers losing their lives each day. Over 4250 have been killed, over 30,000 have been wounded, 13,000 seriously, and an estimated 100,000 Iraqi civilians have lost their lives.

These statistics are mere numbers and do not give us the real picture of those with missing limbs, those blinded, those with troubled minds (post traumatic stress syndrome) and over 100 committing suicide who could no longer live with the soul-chilling experience of having destroyed civilian lives, especially those of innocent children.

Standing on an American battleship, in full air force regalia, President Bush on May 13, 2003 announced "Mission Accomplished!" Such grave miscalculation giving the nation a false hope that the war was over, turned out to be bittersweet to tens of thousands of families who were suffering so much anxiety over the presence and loss of their loved ones in Iraq.

Only the future can relate how we extricate ourselves from the quagmire our "unilateral, preemptive war" has created. .

It is in the context of the next chapter we will get to understand America's exploitive and dehumanizing role in the Middle East and give us perspective on all foreign policy.

"Project for New American Century"

MANY troubling questions arise in the minds of most Americans as to our policies and actions throughout the world. What has happened that we as the mightiest military nation on the globe are so prone to attack other nations and are so insensitive to the human needs of billions of human beings in this world?

How do we rationalize our government aligning with corrupt undemocratic powers in third-world countries, permitting our multi-national corporations profiting from sweatshop labor, and displaying a callous indifference to the needs of the suffering millions in those poor countries?

What justification is there for enacting trade agreements with countries that don't respect our standards of environmental protection or the rights of labor? Each year we suffer trade deficits in the hundreds of billions of dollars. Large nations like China and others, ship inferior goods to our land, and then buy American securities giving them debt leverage to challenge our national and international policies.

Where is the line to be drawn stopping millions of jobs continuously destroyed by "down-sizing" and "out-sourcing" to countries like India and China? What logic is there to say that the workers who have lost their jobs can purchase cheaper goods?

What "national security" protections were involved in our military attacks, on Panama, Grenada, the

Dominican Republic and our expending billions to bolster and uphold the murderous regimes of El Salvador and other Latin American countries?

What is the reasoning behind our right to have thousands of nuclear missiles, along with Russia, France, England, China, India, Pakistan and Israel, for our defense but small countries have no right to so defend themselves?

In these days of modern warfare isn't it the only effective, and **comparable** means of defending their sovereignty?

What have been the hidden economic and political motivations behind the undeclared wars that we have engaged in during the last half of the Twentieth Century and now find us bogged down in the quagmire of Iraq with daily loss of American lives?

There are answers to the foregoing. The problem is that we haven't been able to see the "forest because of the trees." Our minds have focused solely on isolated events that have impacted on our existence. A controlled media, functioning at the behest of corporate entrenched power, has had a self-interest in keeping the people's focus fragmented.

To get rational perspective we must combine our flawed capitalist economic system, our private banking system, our preemptive military doctrine and our predatory globalization ventures all together into a convoluted entity.

This colossal giant of power has been gestating for many years but hadn't taken tangible and covert form until recent time. It encompasses goals inimical to the well being and survival of our nation and the world. It involves United States dominion of the world. It looks beyond mere control of the world. It seeks to own it!

That monstrous entity can now be identified as **"Project for New American Century"**. We need to understand its far-reaching goals, its modus operandi and who are its principal advocates..

It wasn't until the end of the Cold War, when the United States emerged as the only Super-power in the world, that powerful economic forces, and reckless men at the helm of our nation, commenced to entertain empirical plans to exploit and conquer the world.

It had its genesis in the words of President Eisenhower when he forewarned of a "military-industrial complex" that was taking shape in the 1950s. He had these prophetic words to say in January 1961:

> **In the counsels of Government, we must guard against the acquisition of unwarranted influence, whether sought or unsought, by the Military Industrial Complex. The potential for the disastrous rise of misplaced power exists, and will persist. We must never let the weight of this combination endanger our liberties or democratic processes.**

And, some ten years after WWII when he was Commander of all Allied Forces he made this assessment in 1953, at the end of the Korean War, in which 50,000 young Americans died in the purported effort to stem Communism:

> **Every gun that is made, every warship launched, every rocket fired signifies, in the final sense, a theft from those who hunger and are not fed, those who are cold and are not clothed. The world in arms is not spending money alone. It is spending the sweat of laborers, the genius of its**

scientists, the hopes of its children. . . . This is not a way of life at all, in any true sense. Under the cloud of threatening war, it is humanity hanging from an iron cross.

Strange how the very mightiest among us have changes of both mind and heart in later reflection on the roles that they have played. Certainly, this was the case of a famous war hero, Dwight Eisenhower, both as Commander of Allied forces and President of the United States at a later time

An article in **Human Quest,** January-February, 2004 issue, gives us an insight into initial organizations set up to further the purposes of entrenched corporate powers, commercial and financial, in collaboration with the Pentagon.

In 1976 the CPD (Committee on Present Danger) had its origin. Then, in 1988 the CSP (Commission on Security Policies) came into being. And finally in 1997 PNAC (Project for New American Century) was born.

While its chief architect was Paul Wolfowitz, Deputy Secretary for the Pentagon under Rumsfeld, other public personalities making up the vanguard for the monopolistic powers behind the scenes were Vice President Dick Cheney, Richard Perle, Deputy Secretary of Defense under Reagon, Secretary of State Colin Powell, Douglas Feith, undersecretary of defense policy, U. S. Attorney Ashcroft, Karl Rove and others.

Of course, the front man was the nation's President, George W. Bush. He demonstrated an eager willingness to play the messianic head of the **Project for New American Century.**

It would be naïve to not recognize that the behavior of all the foregoing personalities is but the fronts of the corporate conglomerates, financial and non-financial, that are the real arbiters of American policy and action.

On February 3, 2004 Noam Chomsky appeared before the UN Correspondents Association in New York City to receive a special plaque for his outstanding work toward a more just and peaceful world. The plaque identified Chomsky "as the conscious of the people." It was recognition of his courageous and rational thinking, so distinctive throughout the past decades.

Noam Chomsky in his book **Hegemony or Survival: America's Quest for Global Dominance** (2003) documents in precise detail the manipulated strategy during the last half of the 20th Century. Irrespective of what international laws are broken, irrespective of what the costs to both property and lives, U. S. policy has sought global dominance, economically, politically and militarily.

The employment of "preemptive strike" against Iraq based on false contentions and lies have created a quagmire that is dampening considerably the whole "Project for American New Century." We can only witness the unraveling of the Project and prayerfully envision its termination.

A most uncanny analysis of misdirected power and abuse of power is contained in a book that was published in 1939. It is most fitting that it be highlighted in the next chapter.

~ 46 ~
"Power and Morality"

PERHAPS NO BOOK published in the past century so clearly pinpoints the historically abuse of power as a book researched and written by Professor Pitirim Sorokin at Harvard and Walter A. Lunden, Professor of Sociology at Iowa State University. The book, **Power and Morality,** was published in 1939 but is as timely today as it was when it was first published.

The important contribution that these distinguished professors made, and it should be noted that both were learned men with many years of research and writing in the fields of sociology and criminality, was to historically substantiate Lord Acton's classic conclusion "Power corrupts, and absolute power corrupts absolutely"

Covering the past twenty-five centuries of Greco-Roman and Western civilization, they show that to the exact degree that power is exercised, to that same degree criminal behavior is present. The whole spectrum of crime, from bribery and fraud to killing and mass murder, is covered. No aspect, or level of society is untainted by the corrupting influence of power.

Out of the whole research, which cites not only statistics of crime but relates them directly to persons and offices, emerges the irrefutable picture that the tendency toward, and the guilt of, crime are over-whelmingly more prevalent in those who rule than in the ruled.

Although increased power corrupts, whether in industry, finance, or even in institutionalized religions, the most naked and irresponsible display of power is in governments themselves. Here we find that criminality has always exceeded that of the rank and file who have made up the citizenry. Every level of government is affected.

Whereas we readily associate brutality, chicanery and murder with pre-Western despotic rulers, we are blind to the fact that outside of the larger part of the Nineteenth Century, when a reasonable degree of democratic participation existed both economically and politically, the nations of the world have reverted back to a condition of immorality and violence making the bestiality of the past insignificant by comparison.

Despite the fact that this book was written just before WWII and pertained to the devastating war that seemed inevitable, the conclusions of the authors are equally applicable respecting the "corrupting influence of power" in all wars since that time.

Witness what they stated in their introduction to "Power and Morality":.

> Never before in history has the life or death of so many depended upon so very few! The greatest autocrats of the past had but a fraction of the tremendous power held now by a few members of the Politburo or the top leaders of the United States ruling elite.
>
> This dangerous situation naturally raises the momentous question of our time. Can we entrust the fateful decision of war or peace—and through that the "life, liberty and pursuit of happiness" of hundreds of millions of human

beings—to the few magnates of this power? Do they have the wisdom of the serpent and the innocence of the dove necessary to lead us to a lasting peace and a magnificent future?

How timely it is to pose the same serious questions now in 2009 despite the fact that a new cast of world leaders is making the decisions! Sorokin and Lunden sum up their concerns for the future of humanity with these grave forebodings:

> Still mainly tribal governments of politicians, by politicians, and for politicians, today's ruling groups do not display the minimum of intellectual moral and social qualifications necessary for a successful solution of these tremendous tasks. . . Throughout history the moral integrity of powerful governments has been—and still is—too low and their criminality too great to entrust to them the life and well being of mankind.

The authors presented an historically supported thesis that "power corrupts, and absolute power corrupts absolutely". They urgently pleaded, as we should now, demand complete disarmament, fully recognizing the suicidal threat of a thermo-nuclear holocaust. But there was balance in their presentation. They also urged for the adoption of an "Integral" order amongst humankind, premised on love instead of hate.

Although it is specific individuals who exercise corrupt and criminal power, the basic wrong lies with the systems themselves that encourages and allows the exercise of corruption and exploitation. Ultimately, the society, and the world, degenerates into breakdown and conflict.

All levels of organized societies become victims. All are losers. The few have been corrupted by over-participation. The majority is increasingly driven to crime and anti-social conduct because of under-participation.

There is folly and futility to solely concentrate on individuals or groups, however criminal their actions. They appear and disappear with the passing of time but the faulty systems persist through each succeeding generation. Our indictment must focus on the social, economic, financial and political systems **themselves**, which underlie, allow and encourage all levels of injustice, human suffering, hate, terrorism and carnage.

I have presented as clearly as I have been able the diabolical and ruinous power of the Federal Reserve System, the despotic role of private capitalism and the sham of the political system precluding fair elections and the enactment of just laws.

Finally, I have presented as clearly as I have been able the proposal for *novus, ordo seclorum* (a New Order for the Ages). I have blueprinted how with the adoption of a **National Cooperative Commonwealth** we could have a new birth of freedom where the tremendous work capability of the nation could be fully unleashed, with full implementation of human rights, and the widest dispersal of governing power to the sovereign people.

Peace with economic justice is the watchwords. The dynamic formula for major change is enlightenment, proposals and action!

47

Action

WE NOW COMMENCE to deal with steps leading to the achievement of our goals. A critical dynamic should guide our every thought and be solidly embedded in our consciousness. Constantly in our minds must be the unwavering conviction that in the hands of the sovereign citizens is the absolute power to bring about all changes for their betterment.

Every waking morning we should be inspired and energized by what President Lincoln said in his first inaugural address, March 4, 1961:

> **This country with its institutions belongs to the people who inhabit it. Whenever they shall grow weary of existing government, they can exercise their constitutional right of amendment, or their revolutionary right to dismember or overthrow it.**

There is no circumstance or force that can deny the sovereign people the power to take actions or enact proposals that will solve their most serious problems and fulfill their most imaginative aspirations. As we have interspersed throughout this book the only weapon the people need is truth as to the causes of their suffering and injustice, and the legislative enactment of proposals that will eliminate that suffering and injustice.

To quote the outstanding Frenchman, Victor Hugo, "No army can withstand the strength of an idea whose time has come!"

Broad Considerations for Change

Our **first** major consideration is that it is only in the context of the whole society that any individual segment can find solutions to its particular problems. All segments are interdependent and must maintain ties with all other segments in order to survive. In addition each is vulnerable to the universal threats of a polluted environment, the confiscatory taxation of bureaucratic government and the interest-bearing debt of the Federal Reserve System.

Most seriously is the insecurity to every segment of the nation, and the world, when a doctrine of unilateral-preemptive war is recklessly adopted by other nations with imperialistic designs, posing a constant threat of nuclear annihilation?

A book entitled **Sociological Imagination** by C. Wright Mills (1959) covers clearly the folly of any one segment endeavoring to solve its problems by itself. He covered how no individual has security of job until there is universal job security. No one can be solvent until there is national solvency.

The **second** consideration is that it is only in the context of the whole society that sufficient political clout can be rallied to bring about major change. There were times in the past when segments like those in agriculture and labor were of sufficient numbers to spearhead change for the entire society. However, gradually their numbers have dwindled to the point that they no longer can muster sufficient strength to effect universal change.

And the **third** consideration is that it is only in the context of the whole society with all the citizens participating can major change be sustained. There can be no more tragic development than a renovated society being vulnerable prey to ulterior forces, within or without the nation, because of an uninformed citizenry.

The same instability would maintain if those believing in "divine intervention" as the only solution to our problems had their theological fulfillment.

Protest

There is a ground swell of protests throughout the land., largely focused on all the main problems besetting the nation. Tens of millions are protesting the Iraq war in all its tragic dimensions. Equal protest is focused on the economy with millions without work and millions evicted from their homes. The same on the health care system with the sick unable to pay for their prescription drugs, on the young unable to pay for college, and on the nation's children going to bed hungry when the shelves are bulging with food.

Much energy and thought are behind all such protest. And in some cases some results have been achieved. No one can suggest that protest should cease and pay no attention to the suffering and injustice that is involved. Survival itself demands that protest should have its day.

However, mere protest, however warranted, in the long run is largely wasted time. When sufficient people are rallied behind proposals that would break abusive corporate power, which is responsible for the ills mentioned, the ones entrenched **will expose themselves** by opposing the proposals that **would unseat** them.

Exposure of wrong and pursuit of justice are meshed in one effective solitary effort!

Most importantly there would be *esprit de corp* amongst all who seek that better life. There is sustaining effort in the knowledge that achievement is attainable. There is spiritual uplift in working for peace with justice.

Options for Change

In this land there are two basic approaches to enact new laws or meaningful policy. Both are dependent on the political decision-making of the electorate. The efficacy and wisdom of these efforts are directly related to the enlightenment of the people and their vision of a good future for themselves and their children.

Our government is a Representative Republic in which democracy, by the **rule and authority of the people**, can only be realized by the actions of an informed citizenry.

There are, however, political opportunists who subscribe to the philosophy that the citizenry is not astute enough to have their voices paramount in the functioning of government. They hold that those elected have the exclusive role of arbitrarily making all decisions.

There is no recognition that it is "we the people" whose wellbeing, whose lives and whose future are at stake.

Remember what Thomas Jefferson, the most ardent champion of democratic government, stated in reference to the ultimate powers of government:

I know of no safe depository of the ultimate power of society but the people themselves, and

273

if we think them not enlightened enough to exercise their control with a wholesome discretion, the remedy is not to take it from them but to inform their discretion by education.

The sovereign citizens of this nation have two basic approaches to political change. Either sufficient people can be enlightened to pressure the Congress to enact legislation or the people can elect their own candidates who will honestly do the people's bidding.

Realistically, the Congress is crystallized into a pattern of maintaining the status quo of the society and function at the behest of the lobbyists representing the corporate power in the wings. Also, many members are millionaires along with the fact that the majority have stock in the corporate network and feel that they would jeopardize their holdings by economic change.

In 2004, during the race for the presidency, too many people believed if only a new president were elected all the issues of health, education, unemployment, spiraling debt, restoration of international relations, and even the reckless doctrine of "preemptive war" would all be solved.

It was simplicity at its worse. It was the height of stupidity. It was putting political naiveté on a pedestal. It was an absence of rational thinking.

Despite the pervasive power of the main media, radio, TV, Internet, newspapers and magazines, which are despotically controlled by a handful of monopolies, ironically we have them in a bind. In opposing our proposals, which threaten their usurped power, they are **exposing themselves** without **expenditure of effort** on our part.

48

"Inauguration of a Cooperative Commonwealth"

IN THE introduction to my book **A Blueprint for Survival** I mention a most interesting fact relative to the ultimate goals of the Founding Fathers. I refer to a book called, **We, the Other People** edited by Philip. S. Foner, which was published by the University of Illinois Press in 1976.

On July 4, 1879 at a celebration by Chicago Labor a series of resolutions were adopted in favor of the eight-hour day. The resolutions were viewed *"as a vital first step in achieving a fundamental redistribution of wealth that would eventually result in the decline of capitalism and the inauguration of a Cooperative Commonwealth."*

Get this most significant conclusion: *"With realization of this new society, the promises of the original Declaration of Independence would be fulfilled."*

Another pertinent reference is found in a "Declaration of Independence" which was published on July 4, 1895 by David De Leon, leader of the Socialist Labor Party. After citing similar opening phrases of the original Declaration of Independence, and then a list of grievances, the new declaration promised to *"complete the original manifesto through the establishment of the Cooperative Commonwealth.*

"With the triumph of the toilers over their combined despoilers will end class privilege and class rule. Thus would the American Revolution be completed!"

A century has passed since these resolutions were published. Our efforts toward a just and peaceful society are but a belated effort to achieve the ultimate society that was envisioned by our forefathers. What could be more satisfying and inspiring than to be in sync with efforts that would complete the tenets of the "American Revolution"!

Novus Ordo Seclorum

Order for a New Age

EDWABD BELLAMY is best identified with his book **Looking Backward**. However, it is his suppressed book **Equality** that is more pertinent and vital to our efforts. While his critique of private capitalism is uniquely insightful as to its flaws and inequities, it is his proposals for "an integrated economic system coordinating the efforts of all for the common welfare" that is relevant to the society that we envision.

He envisioned a "nationalized industrial system" that step for step replaced the old order for a new order. Pleading for "a new spirit of intelligence" he sounded a tocsin loud and clear:

> **"Face about! . . . Fight forward, not backward! March with the course of economic evolution, not against it. The competitive system can never be restored; neither is worthy of restoring, having been at best an immoral, wasteful, brutal scramble for existence. New issues, demand new answers. It is in vain to pit the moribund system of competition against the young giant of private monopoly; <u>the greater giant of public monopoly must rather oppose it. . . .</u>**

In one short paragraph Bellamy capsulates our whole effort toward that better society.

The capitalists have destroyed the competitive system. Do not try to restore it, but rather thank them for the work, if not the motive, and set about not to rebuild the old village of hovels, but to rear on the cleared place, the temple humanity so long has waited for.

Bellamy never lived to see that "temple" which he envisioned a century ago. From whatever higher spiritual plane he views the happenings that are transpiring on this earth, I am sure that he would find extreme satisfaction in our promotion of a **National Cooperative Commonwealth.**

I am confident also, that he would arise and give a hearty salute to the Prince of Peace who over two thousand years ago formed a "Scourge of Cords and drove the moneychangers out of the temple"!

Bibliography

Adams, Silas Walter, *The Legalized Crime of Banking,* Meador Publishing Coo, Boston, 1958

Beard, Charles A. *An Economic Interpretation of the Constitution of the United States of the United States, Macmillan, 1961*

Beard, Charles A. *President Roosevelt and the Coming of the War, 1941* Yale University Press, New Haven, 1948

Bloom, Allen *The Closing of the American Mind,* Simon & Schuster, NY, 1987

Buchanan, Patrick J. *Churchill, Hitler and the Unnecessary War,* Crown Publishers, New York, 2008

Coogan, Gertrude M. *Money Creators,* Omni Publications,

P. O. Box 216, Hawthorne, California

Congressional Union of Scotland *MONEY—A Christian View,* Glasgow, 1962

Dwinell, Olive Cushing *The Story of Our Money,* Meador, Boston, 1946

Elis, Joseph J. *Founding Fathers,* Alfred A. Knopf, 2000

Federal Reserve Board *The Federal Reserve System: Purposes and Functions, Published periodically by the Federal Reserve Board, Washington, D. C.*

Findley, "Paul *They Dare to Speak Out,* Lawrence Hill & Co., Connecticut,

Fuller, R. Buckminster *Utopia or Oblivion, the Prospects for Humanity,* Bantam Books, 1971

Greider, William *Secrets of the Temple,* Simon & Schuster, 1987

Greider, William *Who Will Tell the People,* Simon & Schuster, New York,1992

Hattersley, C. Marshall *Wealth, Want and War,* The Social Credit Coordinating Center, Yorks, 1937

Herman & Chomsky *Manufacturing Consent,* Pantheon Books, 1988

Hitchens, Christopher, *The Trial of Henry Kissinger,* Verso, London, New York, 2001

Kennedy, Edward E. *The Fed and the Farmer,* published by Edward Kennedy, Pismo Beach, California

King, Martin Luther, Jr. *Where Do We Go From Here, Chaos or Community,* Beacon Press, Boston, 1967

Lernoux, Penny *In Banks We Trust,* Penguin Books, 1984

Lindbergh, Charles A. *Autobiography of Values,* Harcourt Brace Jovanovich, NY, 1977

Locke, John *Treatise on Government*

Malkin, Lawrence *The National Debt,* Henry Holt & Co. N. Y. 1987

Mills, C. Wright *The Power Elite,* Oxford University Press, 1959

Morton, Frederic *The Rothchilds, A Family Portrait,* Curtis (Atheneum) New York, 1962

Mullins, Eustace *The Federal Reserve Conspiracy,* Common Sense, Union, New Jersey, 1954

Paine, Thomas *The Rights of Man*

Pelley, William Dudley, *No More Hunger,* Aquila Press, Noblesville, Indiana

Russell, Bertrand *Political Ideals,* Simon & Schuster, 1964

Soddy, Frederic, *Wealth, Virtual Wealth and Debt,* Omni Publications, Hawthorne, CA, 1961

Sorokin, Pitirim and Walter Lunden, *Power and Morality,* Porter Sargent, Boston, 1959

Stone, Geoffrey R. *Perilous Times,* W. W. Norton, NY and London, 2004

The Report of the National Advisory Commission on Civil Disorders (The Kerner Report) E. P. Dutton & Co. NY, 1968

Thoren and Warner *The Truth in Money Book,* Truth in Money Incorporated, Chagrin Falls, Ohio, 1984

Vickers, Vincent C. *Economic Tribulations,* Omni Publications, Hawthorne, California, 1960

Voorhis, Jerry *Out of Debt, Out of Danger,* Devin-Adaire, New York, 1943

Woodward, Bob *Maestro,* Simon and Schuster, NY, 2000

Zinn, Howard *Declaration of Independence,* Harper Collins, NY, 1990

* * * * *

Senate and House Reports and Hearings United States Government

Hearings before the Select Committee on Nutrition and Human Needs of the United States Senate, Ninetieth Congress, Second Session (1968-1969)

Hearings before the Sub-Committee on Antitrust and Monopoly, Committee on the Judiciary, United States Senate, Eighty-Eighth Congress, on Economic concentration.

Part I: Overall and conglomerate Aspects (1964)

Part II: Mergers and other factors affecting Industry Concentration (1965)

Hearings before Sub-Committee of the Select Committee on small Business, United States Senate, Ninetieth Congress, Second Session on Planning, Regulation, and Competitions Automobile Industry (1968)

Hearings before the Sub-Committee, on Economy in Government of the Joint Economic Committee, Congress of the United States, Ninetieth Congress, Second Session on Economics of Military Procurement (1969)

Hearings on the Impact of Automation on Employment before the Sub-Committee on Unemployment and the Impact of Automation, of the Committee on Education and Labor, House of Representatives, Eighty-Seventh Congress, First Session, (1961)

Hearings before the Sub-Committee on Domestic Finance, of the Committee on Banking and Currency, House of Representatives, Eighty-Eighth Congress, second Session on the Federal Reserve System after Fifty Years, 3 vols. (1964)

A Primer on Money (1964)

Money Facts (1964)

Federal Reserve Directors: A Study of Corporate and Banking Influence by the Committee on Banking, Currency and Housing, House of Representatives, 94th Congress, Second Session, August, 1976

Interlocking Directorates Among the Major U. S. Corporations by Sub-Committee on Reports, Accounting and Management, Committee on Governmental Affairs, United States Senate, January, 1978

Voting Rights in Major Corporations by Sub-Committee on Reports, Accounting and Management, U. S. Senate, January, 1978

Oversight Hearings on Mergers by Sub-Committee on Antitrust, Monopolies and Business Rights, Committee on the Judiciary, U. S. Senate, March 11, 1987

Index

A Blueprint for Survival, 16

ABM TREATY, 237

Abraham Lincoln, 7, 57

Accounting banking system, 37

Accounting System of Banking, 224

Action, 270

AFL-CIO, 79

African-American President, 105

Agency of Consumer Enlightenment, 221

Agency of Scientific Development, 222

Agency of work capability, 215

Agent Orange, 188

Agenda, 21, 137

AIPAC, 246

Al Qaeda, 259

Alexander Hamilton, 42

Aldrick Banking and Currency Committee, 64

Bags of Gold, 26

Bailout of Wall Street, 103

Bankers testify under oath, 77

Banking Currency and the Money Trust, 8

barter, 23

Barter System, 252

Bar Room Ballad, 112

Bilderbergers, 134

Blackened Cinder, 237

Blueprint for Survival, 100, 174

Board of Governors, 75

Break through via Carnage, 187

Bureau of Public Debt, 102

Business Roundtable 180

Central Bank, 62

Central Reserve Assoc., 64

Central banking system, 132

CEOs, 124

Challenge to Crisis, 16

Charles A. Lindbergh, 146

Charles W. McCune, 190

Charles A.. Beard, 249

Chase Manhattan, 174

"chatell slavery", 146

Cheap dollar, 9

Chemical Bank, 174

"Christian Commonwealth", 13

Churchill, Hitler and the Unnecessary War, 254

Citigroup, 104

Civil War, 51

Collaboration with Tyrants, 242

Congressman Lindbergh, 10

Cong. Louis T. McFadden, 14, 151

Congressman Jerry Voorhis, 55

Cong Study Corporate Influence, 73

"cooking of books", 76

Cooperative League, 79

Congressional Record, 114

Congressman Charles Lindbergh, 119

Cong. Louis T. McFadden, 151

Cong. John Rarick, 160

Committee on the Judiciary, 158

Corporate globalization, 136

Corporate mergers, 169

Cost of buying a home, 107

Citigroup, 173

Clifford Hugh Douglas, 191

"Club System", 74

Corner Stones, 204

Common Sense, 240

CPO, 264

C. Wright Mills, 271

Currency and coin, 93

Custodial Care, 234

Debt-free funding, 226

Debt merchants, 26

Defense of the Realm *Act,* 253

Deflation, 98

Demonetize silver, 55

Democracy, issue of money, 131

Democracy 183

Department of Economic Coordination, 213

Determining Individual Worth, 219

Department of the Treasury, 224

Department of Housing, 231

"design science", 222

"dollar" unit-measurement, 29

Domestic Finance Committee, 38

Dr. Federick Soddy, 109

Dollar bill, 116

Dollar bond, 116

"down sizing", 122

Eagle's Eye, 251

Earned claims, 17

Earthwise, 222

Economic Justice and Peace, 236

Edward Bellamy, 276

Einstein, 200

Electgoral College, 182

El Salvador, 243

Eminent Domain, 202

Enrico Fermi, 200

Equally Important, 204

Equal right to education,

Equal right to health care, 209

Equal right to work, 210

Equal right to voice, 210

Equal right to life, 208

Equality, 190

European Feudalism, 197

Farmer's Alliance, 190

Father Couglin, 191

Fannie Mae, 103

Fed. Reserve Bank of Atlanta, 174

Federal Debt, 102, 123

Federal Reserve Act, 156

Federal Reserve Agents, 159

Federal Reserve System, 12

Federal Reserve Notes, 161

"Federal Reserve after 50 years", 79

Fidel Castro, 242

Fifty-three million lives, 14

Five Percent", 111

FMLN, 243

Floor of Congress, 68

Founding Fathers, 44

"fractional reserve", 88

Freddie Mac, 103

Frederick Morton, 60

Funding of the Commonwealth, 212

GATS, 140

George W. Bush, 13

Gen. Smedley Butler, 240

General; Accounting Office,

General Dwight Eisenhower, 254

Gertrude M. Coogan, 64

Global Mind Change, 101

Goldsmith Bankers, 38

goods and services, 30

Gold, 52

Gold standard, 84

Glass-Seagall Act, 174

Globalization, 230

Gramm-Linch-Bliley Act, 174

Great Depression, 10, 154

"Greenbacks", 47

Gutele Schnapper, 61

Hamburg, 63

Hamilton County Mental Health, 121

Head Start, 124

Hegemony or Survival, 246

Henry Ford, 114

Henry S. Reuss (D Wisc) 73

High dollar, 97

Hit Man Perkins, 246

Holland Report, 216

Honorable Carter Glass, 65

H. R. 17140, 160

House Comm. On Banking and Currency, 57

Hugh B. Hester, 251

Human Quest, 264

Hunger in America, 120

ID and Debit card, 228

Imminent danger, 255

Imperial Stretch, 246

IMF and World Bank, 135

Informed citizenry, 168

Informed consent, 255

Inflation, 97

In These Times, 171

Interest-bearing debt, 28

Interest Toll, 102

Iraq, 259

Isotopes, 127

ITTA, 140

Iraq, 259

Japanese internment, 256

Jean-Bertrand Aristide, 245

Jim Tarbell, 246

Joel Bleifuss, 171

John Adams, 44

John Paul Stevens, 182

John Taylor, 44

J. F. Morgan, 103

J, P, Morgan Chase, 173

Judicial Determination, 202

Kofi Annan, 237

Korea, 258

" Labor superior to capital", 49

Lobbyists, 180

Lokas Journal, 233

Mayer Amschal Rothschild, 60

Media conglomerates, 125

Media Monopoly, 181

medical insurance, 122

medium of exchange, 25

Merit share, 215, 219

Medicaid, 124

Merit share, 215, 219

Michael's Journal, 192

Military Industrial Board, 263

Minneapolis Fed. Reserve Bank, 62

M. M. Warburg and Co., 62

Money Creators, 64

Money Facts, 38

"Money Trust", 67

Monetizing citizen's assets,173

Muscle Shoals, 114

My Country at War, 8

NAFTA, 140

National Association of Manufacturers, 74

Nagasaki, Hiroshima, 254

Natural Heritage, 199

National Cooperative Commonwealth, 14

National Bank Act, 51,56

National Operating Credit, 228

Nationalizing Foreign Assets, 229

National Cooperative Commonwealth, 193

9-inch ball of gold, 109

911 Commission, 260

Nobel Prize in Chemical Bonding, 128

No More Hunger, 13, 193

Nonproliferation Treaty, 237

Novou Ordo Seclorum, 276

Nuclear missiles, 262

Olive Cushing, 70

"On a Cross of Gold", 56

One's Castle, 234

Options for change, 276

Open Market Committee, 90

OPEC, 140

Out of Debt, Out of Danger, 55

"out sizing", 12

Palestinians, 245

Participatory democracy, 211

Patrick J. Buchanan, 254

Paul Warburg, 62

Pauillas Wedding, 144

People's Wealth, 201

Perilous Times, 257

Persian Gulf War, 259

Polish Corridor, 252

Political Parties, 178

Political Convention, 179

Power and Morality, 266

President Jackson, 45-+

President Lincoln, 47, 167

"Public Trust", 72

Primer on Money, 91 94

Proportionate equity, 170

Private banking control, 173

Political Slavery, 176

Proportionate Representation, 181

Proposals, 189

Principles of Incorporation, 193

Planned Economy, 195

Proportionate Ownership, 201

Preamble to the Constitution, 206

President Mosedegh, 244

Pres. Hugo Chavez, 244

Pres. Franklin Roosevelt, 249

President Roosevelt and the Coming of the War, 1941, 250

Project American New Century, 261

Proportionality, 256

Protest, 272

Philip S. Toner, 275

Quality of Life, 205

Ralph Nader, 135

Real Wealth, 128

Realty share, 215

ROBERT WHITE, 243

Regime Change, 247

Reginald McKenna, 83

Regime Change, 247

Rep. Charles Lindbergh, 6

Rep. Wrioght Patman, 78

Rep. Conzales (D Texas), 80

"Responsive Politics", 177

Resolutions 244 and 338, 245

Robert L. Owens, 64

ROBERT WHITE, 243

Rothschild's, 60

Royal Swedish Academy,. 128

Sage of Menlo Park, 113

Salvador Allende, 244

Santa Clara County Case. 171

Scourge of Cords, 29

Science and Technology, 184

Senate Comm. on Banking and Currency, 64

Senator Huey Long, 191

Senator Russell Long, 177

Seymour Harris, 81

Sherman and Clayton Acts, 124

Skill rate, 219

Social Credit, 191

Social Justice, 191

Sociological Imagination, 271

Soddy's important books, 121,128

Sorokin and Lunden, 266

Soviet Union, 14

State of the World, 137

Summary, 143

Sovereign Powsr, 206

Super Highway of Information, 186

"system engineering", 127

Taxing Power, 202

The Aldrick Monetary Commission, 70

Tennessee River, 115

Tina Loebe, 63

The Danger of Money, 129

The Eagles Eye, 16

The Enigma of Money, 18

The Devil Theory of War, 238

The Fed Res. System, its origin and growth, 63

The "Fed". 60

"The Greatest Crime in History", 151

The Human Tragedy, 120

"The Phantom Devil", 238

The Price of Truth, 257, 277

"The Lone Eagle", 67

The Story of Money, 70

The Tounsend Plan, 191

The "Region", 62

The New York Times, 113, 118

Third World, 137

There Is a Way, 16, 100

Thomas Jefferson, 44, 94 113, 206

Thomas Edison, 94,113

Trade Treaties. 139

Treasury gold, 92

Tufts University, 120

True Wealth, 203

Tyler Kent, 252

"unearned" dollars, 32

Unearned Profit, 196

Unnatural entities, 169

Upton Sinclair, 191

Upton Sinclair, 191

U. S. Chamber of Commerce, 74

US Treasury, 158

Usurers, 51

Vampiristic Interest, 101

Victor Hugo, 270

Vietnam, 258

VX nerve agent, 123

Washington Spectator, 177

Wealth, Virtual Wealth and Debt, 109, 127, 225

William Dudley Pelley, 193

William Jennings Bryan, 57

Willis Harman, 101

World War II, 248

WTO. 140

Your Country at War, 119

The author, 93 years young, resides with his feline partner, "Reeka," in Noblesville, Indiana. He currently is working on his sixth book, *A Reluctant Heretic.*